# The Nana

'In these pages, we see Taylor's remarkable gift of elevating the ordinary to something special, something poetic, even ...'
*Irish Independent* on *The Women*

'It's like sitting and having a big warm blanket wrapped around you ...'
*Cork Today with Patricia Messinger* on *Tea for One*

**For more books by Alice Taylor, see obrien.ie**

Alice Taylor grew up during the 1940s and 1950s on a farm along the Cork-Kerry border. She remembers the farm women coping and managing to sustain a good living in tough circumstances. Their main focus was to keep their family fed, clothed and educated, but their resourcefulness enabled them to weave a life that enriched everyone around them. They had skills honed by previous generations whose resilience inspired them and taught them a respect for the land, the environment and family heritage.

# The Nana

**Alice Taylor**

**Photographs by Emma Byrne**

First published 2022 by Brandon,
an imprint of The O'Brien Press Ltd.
12 Terenure Road East, Rathgar, Dublin 6
D06 HD27, Ireland.
Tel: +353 1 4923333 Fax: +353 1 4922777
Email: books@obrien.ie
Website: obrien.ie
The O'Brien Press is a member of Publishing Ireland.

ISBN 978-1-78849-386-4

10 9 8 7 6 5 4 3 2 1
25 24 23 22

Printed and bound in Poland by Bialostockie Zaklady Graficzne S.A.
The paper used in this book is produced using pulp from managed forests.

## Dedication

Remembering Maureen,
whose mission in life was
to inspire and encourage

# Contents

Introduction

# Meeting the Nanas

When you opened the door from our small quarry-tiled front hall into the low-ceilinged parlour her calm, appraising gaze met you across the room. Her serene presence reached out from her picture and made you feel welcome. This was Grandmother Taylor and even though she had died years before I was born I grew up feeling that she was a comforting presence in our house. My grandfather had died when my father was sixteen, then she and Dad had run the farm together. It must have been a very amicable partnership because after her death at the age of sixty, he had taken her photograph to Cork, which was no mean journey at that time, and got her portrait painted. Money was a scarce commodity in rural Ireland of the 1930s and many years later, curious as to the motivation and the details behind this unusual undertaking, I enquired how much this portrait had cost back then. My father smiled and informed me in farmer's language, 'The price of an in-calf heifer.' In an effort to equate that cost in today's world I recently enquired from a local farmer as to how much money that would be nowadays and was told, 'For a good one, about two thousand euro.' A sizeable sum! But what a visionary investment by my father for our family, and because of it my grandmother lived on in all our lives, as indeed so did her tradition of music and song that she had brought into the austere Protestant lineage of the family she had joined on marriage.

My maternal grandmother, on the other hand, lived just back the road and was our living family matriarch. She was known as Nana Ballyduane, taking her name from the townland where she lived until the grand old age of ninety-eight. From there she was very much a force to be reckoned with right up to the end of her days.

Nana Ballyduane might remind you of the iconic picture of the Peig Sayers-type of Irishwoman, dressed in black, sitting by the fire. She certainly was not a 'hugs and cuddles' Nana, but kept us at arm's length, feeling that her role in our lives was to 'straighten us out and straighten us up'. She was of her time. These two women were the grandmother bookends of my childhood, one from her picture on the wall and the other from a few miles back the road from where she beamed like a far-ranging control tower.

My generation has gone through three reigns of Nanas – our own grandmothers, our mothers who were Nana to our children, and ourselves, now Nana to our children's children. In my case this spans from Nana Ballyduane's birth in 1860 up to the present day. What a long perspective we have on the role of Nana.

But in order to ascertain a broader view on the influence of the Irish Nana it was necessary for me to go further afield than my own experience. So views on the Nanas in our extended family were sought and then it was time to hear about the Village Nanas and some from further afield.

It was interesting to discover that our remembrances of our Nanas are largely very positive, which would lead one to the belief that the grandchild–Nana relationship is a special inter-generational comfort blanket.

This contradicts Shakespeare's observation that 'The evil that men do lives after them, the good is oft interred with their bones.' Not so with Nanas! Not so. The Irish Nana is very lovingly remembered for all kinds of different reasons and she is a huge part of our national culture. Nana, as well as having a unique position in the family, also has it in society. In Italy, the 'Nonna' embodies, in particular, all the expert recipes from previous generations before cookbooks were on our bookshelves; they were and are the repositories of a wonderful and ancient cooking tradition. The Irish Nana, too, occupies a special space, though, probably due to famine and poverty, not so much for cooking, though there are wonderful traditions which she will recall and practice, but in the context of storytelling and music, and especially in her knowledge of family and local history. To the Irish

Nana, family roots were and are of huge importance. She is the living history book.

Some of these Nanas were the bridges between generations, linking us back to our ancestors. Often they were the family genealogists, who told us who we were and where we came from. They had an in-depth knowledge of the extended branches of the family tree with whom they kept in touch and could trace their genealogy back through the generations, believing that our roots were important, and if we did not know where we came from, we did not know where we were going. Some of them were earthed in another time and brought a sense of tribal belonging into their grandchildren's world. Their values were of a thriftier, more frugal and environmentally caring era, and they endeavoured to hand on that creed.

We have a huge variety of grandmothers. The lovable, cuddly grandmother, the 'do as you're told' grandmother, the demonstrative grandmother, the cranky grandmother, the austere 'children should be seen and not heard' grandmother, and the one who brightened up your life and made the world a kinder place. Grandmothers come in many formats. They are afforded many titles, varying from Grandmama, Grandma, Granny, Gran, Nan, or the more Irish rural Nana or Nanna, and each name conjures up a different image.

Some women are natural mothers and grandmothers and take to those roles like ducks to water. Born with an abiding maternal instinct, mothering is second nature to them.

Others go with the flow and learn on the job, while still others are slightly overwhelmed by the immensity of the tide of responsibility and constantly struggle to keep their heads above water. I think that I come into this last category. With the advent of becoming a grandmother, these waters calmed a little and there is now more time to appreciate and be aware of what in previous years may have been perceived as very demanding and challenging.

Of course, Nanas do occupy a special position. As one Nana told me, 'It's the best of all worlds because you have all of the pluses and none of the minuses.' Isn't that a lovely situation to be in? The grandchildren may come and wreck the house, but at the end of the day they go home and then Nana is back to her orderly self-catering solo living. Nanas have the luxury of being able to indulge their grandchildren, knowing this will not become the norm, because in the heel of the hunt the creation of boundaries in the children's world is the responsibility of the parents. But Nana, if she so desires, can also be stern and uphold strict standards when needed, but again this is not an everyday requirement. So, this is one of the great freedoms in being a Nana.

To be afforded an opportunity to view a grandmother though the eyes of a small child is to get an insight into this unique child–grandmother relationship. John Moriarty, that amazing Kerry visionary and writer, writes about this in one of his books. John was home on holiday on the family farm in Kerry from Canada, where he lectured in the University of Manitoba. It was Good Friday, and while the rest of the family went to the local church for the Easter ceremonies, John and his little niece, who was about six years old, remained at home taking care of a cow that was due to calve. As John and this little girl watched the calf emerge from the cow, the child turned to John and informed him with assurance that she too had come out of her Mammy's tummy, and when John asked her where her mother had come from he was confidently told, 'Oh from Nana's tummy, of course!', but when he queried as the where Nana had come from, the child, looking amazed at his profound lack of knowledge, assured him with absolute conviction, 'Oh, Nana was always there.' To this little girl a world without her Nana was inconceivable. Nana was the back wall of her world. There simply was no life before her Nana.

Traditionally, some Nanas lived in the family home and were part of daily life, and some lived next door or down the street, where a child could run for comfort if things got out of hand at home. If you lived in a city, you might have a grandmother in a village or town, or on a farm down the country where you spent your summer holidays and experienced a whole different world. Sometimes grandchildren from abroad came home on holidays to their Irish Nana and were introduced to their family roots and to a very different way of life. My niece Lisa, who grew up in England, discovered another world on coming back to visit her Nana in our family farm in Lisdangan.

Some years ago when book-signing in Dublin I also came across a number of Dubs, who, when I enquired why they were buying this book based on country living, told me they had a Kerry, Mayo or Galway grandmother and had spent all their summer holidays on a farm down the country, and had loved it. And now in adulthood these people, because they had such good memories of their childhood holidays, recalled those days with great warmth and wanted to revisit that world. They recalled with gratitude the grandmothers who had made those holidays possible – and usually it was the grandmother who was prepared to take responsibility and look after these grandchildren for long summer holidays, though grandad also played his part. At the time, the children took all of this for granted, but now years later came the appreciation and a loving remembrance of their grandmother and that experience. These adults now felt a huge debt of gratitude.

Those grandmothers were the stay-at-home, working-on-the-farm grandmothers, who are now no longer part of Irish life as farming has changed. Today's grandmothers are no longer at home on the farm – both children and grandmothers are now holidaying in other places. Long ago, though, their presence in the home solved the problem of who would hold the baby and who would mind Nana. Now the baby is in a crèche and Nana is in a nursing home.

But how the grandmother fitted into the family circle depended a lot on the dynamics within the family. If those dynamics were not harmonious, it was the grandchildren who missed out. Sometimes it might have been the mother's mother who was the one more involved with the grandchildren, and this could be because grandmothers felt more at ease expressing opinions on child-rearing to their own daughters rather than to daughters-in-law. Though this might not always be the case, of course, and when at book signings I come across a daughter-in-law buying a book for her mother-in-law, I might sometimes pass the comment, 'You must be a great daughter-in-law', and the return comment is usually, 'I have a great mother-in-law.' It works both ways. But to the children it matters little which side of the family their grandmother comes from, and if the overall family dynamics are comfortable the grandmother–child relationship benefits the children enormously.

In the racing world the 'dam' is the maternal anchor through which the bloodline is traced as it is regarded as the most generative. It is often, apparently, the maternal more than the paternal genes that dictate the psyche of the offspring. The human species may also inherit many of our family traits from our grandmothers, and, irrespective of what we may like to think, some of the ways we are and how we function comes from our family gene pool.

Sometimes, however, the grandmother role can be filled by a loving, kindly neighbour or family friend, and this bond can be very enriching to both parties. These women who may sometimes have no grandchildren of their own can become much-loved adopted Nanas. John O'Donoghue, the Connemara poet and philosopher, wrote about an elderly, kindly neighbour whom he loved dearly – and one evening on coming home from school, he was met with the news that she had died suddenly. He felt his first huge sense of loss as if one of the roots of his world had gone. Sometimes in the life of a child it is the death of a grandmother that first introduces them to the experience of dying. One grandchild told me that to her this event was of such earthshaking importance that she felt that it should be on the Six o'clock News. I myself was twenty when I heard of the death of Nana Ballyduane, with whom I did not have a deep, loving relationship, but I sat down and cried, remembering the nights when she and I, alone together aboard her large, comfortable feather bed, had sailed off into the world of nod as she had taught me her special prayers.

As I begin this book, I feel a queue of these wise women looking over my shoulder. I hope to give them a voice – and hopefully amongst these pages you may find memories of your own Nana and little reminders of her way of life.

*Grandmother Taylor.*

*The open farm kitchen fire, which was cooker, home heating, water warmer, Nana's corner and the heart of the home.*

fire and eased out all our wrinkles. If not handled with caution it could be a dangerous lad!

*Before walk-in wardrobes, this chest of drawers, known as the 'tall boy', was where all foldable clothes were stored.*

*Most Nanas had a set of good china brought forth for the Stations and special visitors.*

Before liquidisers became part of the kitchen, the humble mincer did the needful. But the mincer required much more physical effort. The items went in the top and the handle was turned to grind them through a series of iron discs and out the spout at the front.

The little skillet pot, used for cooking delicacies over the open fire. Mine is now a water supply for the birds in the garden.

*Brass candlesticks were used for the Station Mass and for wakes.*

Chapter One

# The Homemakers

We were bacon, cabbage and spuds children, as indeed were many generations before us. In later years this fare may well have been regarded with some disdain as unimaginative food for the peasants. However, long-ago Nanas kept their families strong and healthy on it and when the potato crop failed we died by the thousand or were forced to emigrate on coffin ships. No wonder then that our Nanas treated the 'royal spud' with the respect it deserved. They oversaw the cutting of the seed potatoes from Golden Wonders, Kerr's Pinks, and Aran Banners into '*sceallán*' and rejecting the '*sceallóg*' which were termed 'blind' as they did not have the necessary productive eye for sprouting new life. The cutting of the *scealláns* was timed so that planting the potatoes could begin from St Patrick's Day onwards and the aim then was not to have 'cuckoo spuds', as late planting was ironically termed. Back then we children had a little verse that we quoted as we waited eagerly to catch sight of the early swallows and to hear the first call of the cuckoo:

> The cuckoo comes in April
> And sings his song in May
> In the middle of June he plays his tune
> And July he flies away.

So if you were planting your spuds to the call of the cuckoo you were really running behind schedule and deemed to be planting 'cuckoo spuds', which were not as tasty as spuds planted earlier.

Children were shown the correct procedure of planting potatoes by a Nana who knew exactly what to do as she too had inherited this knowledge from her Nana. It is not surprising that Jean-Francois Millet's famous painting *The Angelus*, like his other works, incorporates a strong female presence out in the fields. Women shared the farm work, as he shows. In Ireland they also led the way on Rogation Days when the blessing of the crops with holy water took place, thus uniting the natural and the divine to bless the land and ensure a good harvest, and food on the table. The children, of necessity, were brought along to help and to learn. These skills were soon mastered by the young – the correct spacing of the 'sceallán*s*' into little beds of dung brought from outside the cow houses (dung from the hen house was deemed unsuitable), and then laid out along the drills. I remember long, cold days with my siblings, on our hands and knees, slowly making our way up the long field that was the bread basket of the house because in it all that was to sustain us for the year ahead was planted. That was the time for us young ones to apply our neighbour's philosophy of 'Head down, arse to the wind and keep going.' It certainly cultivated our tenacity and 'stickatitness', and was undoubtedly good for flexibility and fitness too.

When the time came for picking the potatoes we children were also part of the work team, and I still remember the sense of wonder that one small *sceallán* we had planted months previously had blossomed into this shower of round, white potatoes now erupting up through the brown earth behind the plough. Nana was then the best judge of how good the potato return was, and if the first tasting got her stamp of approval, then all was well for the year ahead. She had been down this road many times and so was a tried and tested expert on potato quality. Before these potatoes were pitted for the winter, it was often the Nana who came out in the morning to dig the potatoes for that day's dinner from a drill left unharvested for that purpose. Many grandchildren carry fond memories of their Nana making 'pandy' for them – this was made with a big, soft, floury spud mashed up with butter and warm milk, and was a soothing comfort-food that slipped down many a sore throat or into an upset stomach with effortless ease. Even now when I am recovering from a 'flu or any ailment, I still find that a warm mashed spud can bring me right. Nana also made colcannon by mixing chopped kale and cabbage water, which was full of vitamins, through this pandy, rendering it very flavoursome. This colcannon was made in a little skillet pot, which was a very small version of its larger cousin that was used for the boiling of the bacon, cabbage and spuds, but the little skillet was preserved for making delicate niceties. A traditional song was written about it, sung by many performers, but made famous by Mary Black and the Black Family:

> …Oh weren't them the happy days
>> When troubles we knew not
>> And our mother made colcannon
>> In the little skillet pot.

I now have a Nana skillet pot hanging off a tree in the garden and the little birds perch on the rim and have a drink, and a blackbird dives in and uses it as a bird-bath, sending out a shower of spray while he is in action.

And when Nana was bringing in the spuds for the dinner, she would also cut heads of cabbage growing in the same field and so arrive in the kitchen carrying the makings of the dinner for the day with her. Already in a large timber barrel in a cool room off the kitchen were sections of salted bacon waiting to be hauled out and landed into a large, cast-iron black pot and hung over the fire to boil. Once the bacon was cooked, the cabbage, which had been well washed to evict the numerous little tenants harbouring within, was then plunged into the boiling salted bacon water to cook and absorb the flavours. This supply of bacon too had come under Nana's capable supervision because it was often she who had taken care of the mother pig who had produced the young. If one of the litter of bonhams was a bit weak and unable to hold its own amongst the other stronger piglets, it was known as the *'íoctar'*, the runt of the litter. It was then allocated a butter box beside the fire where Nana, from her chimney-corner chair, took care of it and helped to sustain it with a large feeding bottle, sometimes a whiskey bottle, full of milk, and with a teat attached. If the teat weakened due to the strengthening jaws of the bonham, Nana replaced it with a strong, black rubber one, better able to withstand the growing jaw pressure. Pigs were fed on crushed oats to which was added kitchen waste – the 'pigs' bucket' was the receptacle in farm kitchens for all kinds of leftovers. These pigs were the staple meat supply for the household. In our family it was Grandmother Taylor who taught my father the required expertise needed for the 'killing of the pig', and Nana Ballyduane who taught my uncle. This was a challenging undertaking, but these women had mastered the skill of doing the needful as humanely as possible. Their parents had endured the Famine, and these Nanas did not shrink when the need arose to do whatever needed to be done for survival. As in the world of nature, the provision of food for their family was of paramount importance, and the Nanas stood shoulder-to-shoulder with the men in that endeavour. I remember Nana Ballyduane expertly caring for sick animals and skilfully supervising the safe delivery of a valuable calf or foal, and also being in charge of farm finances and wielding a firm hand when it came to its management.

Despite being deprived of inheritance rights, women still carried huge clout on the ground, especially in the farming world. The Nana embodied the essence of that lifestyle and she passed it all on to the next generation. Links between generations were hugely important, especially in homemaking and farming life. Our Nana was born in 1860 but the family tradition goes further back as eight generations of our family have lived on the same farm, which is a long time but not uncommon.

Following the killing of the pig came the filling of the puddings and each family had a closely guarded recipe handed down within the family from the Nana. In our family, Nana Ballyduane directed this operation and left us in no doubt as to how this procedure should be carried out. Filling the puddings was a marathon task which commenced with the chilly undertaking of washing the pudding casings, which, disgusting as it may sound, were actually the guts of the pig. These had to be washed and rewashed endlessly, at a time when there was no water on tap in the homes, so this necessitated long hours of standing in the river to wash the guts in the flowing water. When the guts were clear white and almost transparent, and the whole lot looked and felt like a pan of slithering eels, it was then time to scrape them even cleaner in preparation for the filling of the puddings. The small intestine became the sausages and the large one the black pudding. There were white and black puddings to be filled, and the main ingredient for the black pudding was the boiled blood of the pig. Today, with black pudding on the menu of many top-class Irish restau-rants, we should salute the Nanas whose imaginative inge-nuity created and preserved these recipes. Back then they had no liquidisers or food processors, only the simple iron mincer which was firmly attached to the end of the kitchen table to grind up the cooked liver and the lights (the lungs), and also through the mincer went the boiled belly of the pig. Strictly speaking, all this could be regarded as offal, but in that world nothing was wasted and all this was minced, then mixed together with onions, breadcrumbs and other bits and pieces that were part of the favoured recipe. Within this mincer were different-shaped discs which determined the size and consistency of whatever came out of it. In our house, if a particular-sized disc happened to be missing, it might be necessary to go back the road to Nana Ballyduane who ran a more disciplined house than ours and always had everything to hand when needed. Attaching the mincer to the table had to be done with determination, firmness and accuracy as an insecure, dancing mincer could result in a crash-landing on the floor, with catastrophic consequences. I can still recall the grinding sound of the mincer as, with the determined turning of the handle, the gristly remnants extracted from the melted fat from inside the pig were forced through its iron innards. The resulting minced concoction was then mixed with all kinds of spices and herbs as directed by Nana, until after many tastings and samplings it was deemed to have reached the required flavour and consistency.

Then came the actual filling of the puddings. The front of the mincer had an attachment called a 'filler' put on it and onto this went the end of the pudding casing. The filling was then propelled into the casing. Gradually a long ring of pudding formed, which at a certain point was cut into chosen lengths, and the ends tied firmly with strong cord. When a large amount of these puddings had accumulated, they were then plunged into a big black pot of boiling water over the fire. Fishing the boiled puddings out of the pot was an exercise requiring extreme caution to avoid being scalded, so a long stick was used to lift them out. They were then threaded onto the handle of a brush and bridged across the backs of two *súgán* chairs to cool. Big stacks of these puddings were made, because, as well as fulfilling our own needs, we also took a supply of puddings and fresh pork-steaks around to all the neighbours – and they in turn did likewise when they killed their pig. The Nanas also directed operations when the butchered pig, after the required length of hanging time, had to be salted. She gave instructions as to the correct quantity of salt and the precise amount of water to be added to the large timber barrel which was the final resting place for the pickled pig.

A change from bacon on the menu was occasionally provided by the introduction of roast cockerels, flocks of which roamed around the yard – and whose necks Nana had no problem in wringing when the necessity arose. Some of these she boiled to create her special chicken broth, which she believed was a cure-all and could raise Lazarus from the dead! In the autumn months, she dispatched my uncle to the bog to shoot snipe and grouse and other wild game that she believed held cures for cleansing the blood and for undiagnosable complaints. When the season was right, she was delighted if a cock pheasant came her way, as pheasant was judged to have many health benefits. She fancied herself as being more medically attuned than our local doctor – and had no problem of making him aware of the fact. Unfortunately, for her, there was no river flowing through her farm and so it was up to my father to supply her fresh trout requirements, which he did with certain grin of satisfaction on his face.

Every day Nana made big cartwheels of brown bread, a skill that she passed on to my mother. They both claimed that the secret of making good brown bread lay in the quality of the sour milk available. In the morning, once the cows were milked, a bucket of fresh milk was brought in for use in the house before the churns of milk went off to the creamery, where the cream was extracted to make butter and cheese, and then the skim milk came back to the farm and was used to feed the young calves and pigs.

At the end of the day the leftover house milk was set aside in an earthenware crock or enamel bucket to go sour for baking. A wary eye was kept on it with an occasional stir and when it was deemed to have reached the right maturity it was ready for the job on hand. Weighing scales were not then part of the common culinary equipment, and Nana used a saucer to dole out the required amounts of brown and white flour, into which she measured bread soda with a spoon, and then the sour milk was carefully poured into the mixture. When it was judged to be of the right consistency, it was kneaded into a pliable lump in a baking pan and finally flattened out into the required shape. The making of bread always seemed to bring a sense of fulfilment and tranquility to the bread maker, and while this was in process the bastable was hanging over the fire warming up for the forthcoming baking; and the bastable cover was laid on the fire to bring it to the required heat. Once the cake was ready, a shake of flour was sprinkled into the bastable and then the cake, which was shaped to the same size as the bastable base, was eased in and the hot cover put in place. The outer edge of the cover was then hedged around with glowing red sods of turf, ensuring an even bake. A red-hot turf fire, with the flames whipping between the sods and slowly turning to a red glow was judged to be the best for the baking of brown bread – and also for producing the most gorgeously flavoured toast. Bread toasted on a glowing turf fire slowly turned a golden brown while absorbing the aromatic whiff of the bog, resulting in a crackling, flavoursome mouthful, covered with delicious butter. Toasting forks to do this from a safe distance were fashioned by a resourceful Nana from a strand of creamery wire, which was flexible enough to be shaped into giant forks.

As the cake baked, a lovely smell of baking filled the kitchen and sometimes wafted up the chimney – and even out in the garden and yard you would know by the smell when baking was going on in the house. As the result of years of experience, Nana knew exactly when to swing the crane forward off the fire, lift the sods and take the cover off the bastable with the tongs, and then ease out the baked cake, which she sometimes wrapped in a damp tea towel or flour bag and stood on the window sill to cool. Sometimes another brown cake immediately followed into the bastable and occasionally what we called a 'sweet cake' was made, and that had currants, raisins, sugar and cream. When the apple trees were laden in autumn, Nana made large apple cakes, and as these baked you could smell and hear the apples and sugar gurgling together in the bastable. When the apple cake was lifted out, we children gathered around the bastable with spoons to help ourselves to the sticky, toffee-like substance adhering to the bottom of the bastable where the apple syrup and sugar had congealed. If a loaf of 'shop bread', as we called it, came into the house it was used sparingly, and if any scraps happened to be left over, a bread-and-butter pudding was concocted. The recipe for this varied according to the availability of ingredients and the whims of the maker, but the stale bread was usually layered between fruit and sugar and smothered in hot custard. If you were lucky it might be served with cream.

The flour used in this daily bake had come from the local grain-and-flour merchant, and the flour bags in which it came were known as 'bageens' and were destined for reincarnation into a multiplicity of uses by a resourceful Nana. The bags were made of very good quality material and came in different sizes, depending on the amount of flour ordered. These bags had great potential for other uses around the house. When empty, they were well-washed and then draped over the bushes and bleached for long periods of time in an effort to erode the lettering imprinted on them by the mill, which gave evidence of the fact they had a former life prior to the one planned by Nana! Sometimes she succeeded in fading out the printing to a faint inscription. Nevertheless, our tablecloths, sheets, pillow cases, aprons and, indeed, sometimes our dresses all told the story of their previous life. It did not bother Nana if one of our dresses had the details of the flour mill emblazoned across our fronts or bottoms! Maybe in this she was ahead of her time?

While one flour bag made a pillow case, it took four large ones to make a sheet. Lying between two of these sheets was a pleasurable experience as they had a soft, pleasing touch and they somehow succeeded in being cool in summer and warm and comforting in winter. In the bed over these sheets came the Dripsey and Foxford woollen blankets, which were often gifted by mothers to their daughters when they were setting up their own homes; then over the blankets, like a thatched roof, came the all-encompassing patchwork quilt, some lined with wool or red flannel. Sometimes a quilt could span the generations. When the sheets, due to constant use, began to show signs of wear and tear, a resourceful Nana applied her scissors down the middle and 'turned' them by doing a middle-to-sides job with her sewing machine. Thus she extended their life-span and when they finally reached their journey's end she cut them up and turned them into cleaning and polishing cloths. Her creed in life was 'mastering the art of making do'.

Our Nana was certainly not into high fashion and when she came to my mother's rescue in dressmaking for her five granddaughters, she believed that all that was required was the covering of bodily parts. We finished up with a straight-down garment with a gap at the top for the head and two gaps at the sides for the arms. As children, we did not question her seamstress skills, but as we grew little older and more discerning, we felt like protesting. But we knew that there was no point as Nana did not entertain protestations. However, in later years when I viewed Mary Quant's designs on the catwalk I thought that maybe our Nana was on the ball! And this year as I watched the Cheltenham races I noticed one fashionable racing pundit sported a coat with a contrasting colour strip addition along the bottom – I smiled, remembering our disgust when Nana came up with this solution to cover fast-growing legs beneath shrinking coat lengths!

Our Nana was not into knitting, but there was no short-age of other Nanas around who were dedicated knitters and were delighted to come to our rescue in closing the toe or turning the heel of a sock begun in school, where we also mastered the art of top stitch, running stitch and tacking in our sewing classes. These skills were considered very impor-tant. Different Nanas had different skills, and they often gathered in each other's houses or in their daughters' homes for a chat while practising their particular skills. Common to all was the ongoing need for darning, as socks and jumpers were hand-knit and children were mostly out in the fields where elbows, toes and heels, assisted by briars, regularly made a breakthrough. To this day, I love darning and find it a particularly soothing pursuit as there is something infi-nitely satisfying in the lacing of the darning needle across the threads and the final closing of the gap. Every night my mother and Nana spent hours darning and maybe they too found it a calming and soothing exercise after the hard, demanding physical work then involved in running a house and farmyard. Likewise, if I am half bothered by life, I find that sewing soothes my soul − and maybe this too was the case with our Nanas who pursued the accomplishments of sewing, knitting, quilting, patchwork and lace-making, all of which had the hidden bonus of adding time for meditative tranquility to the end of their busy, hard-working, home-making days.

# Chapter Two

# Nana Back the Road

She died in 1958 at the grand old age of ninety-eight when I was twenty, so my first twenty years were Nana Ballyduane's last twenty. Born in 1860, she was the first generation after the Great Famine, so was birthed into an Ireland still reeling from the experience of extreme hunger. One can only wonder what impact being raised by parents still traumatised by that terrible experience had on their children. My memory of her is of a force of nature one did not trifle with and who was upright and formidable right up to her final days. To be honest, I was half-scared of her, as she sat in her chair by the open fire and issued orders that one would not dream of disobeying. I dutifully complied with every instruction and expectation as she pinned a piercing eye on me and cracked me into action. Back at home my mother was easygoing, so one could dawdle around and avoid jobs, but not so with Nana because with her there was no getting away with anything. To add to my problem, she considered me to be a bit useless as I was into film stars and reading romantic stories, and to her this was a total waste of time – and out of all order. So when I was dispatched back the road to her on what was supposed to be holidays, she tried to straighten me out and turn me into someone useful and industrious, which meant that we were not exactly singing from the same hymn sheet.

However, there was one big plus for me when holidaying with Nana. This was her large tin box of cream-crackers which were kept on a table just inside her bedroom door. I loved her cream-crackers, as we never had such luxuries at home, and often during the day stole up into her bedroom and helped myself, probably considering them some recompense for all the hardships that she was inflicting on me – but there was also a certain amount of guilt attached to stealing her cream-crackers that I eroded by considering them a balance in a relationship in which she held the whip hand. She never said a thing about it. Maybe she too felt it was an evening-out of an imbalance.

Her bedroom had originally been the parlour of the house and had a large sideboard along the back wall and an impressive marble fireplace on another wall, and all these walls were painted a deep royal blue. At some stage, Nana had turned this parlour into her own domain and it somehow reflected her personality with its dark blue walls, solid fireplace and large black iron bed with its solid brass knobs.

This room, in an indefinable way, reflected to me who she was – dark, deep, complex and formidable. My Nana definitely did not belong in the feminine fluffy pink boudoir to which I aspired, having seen such things in a glossy Hollywood magazine.

As I grew older and got to know more about her, I discovered that she was a complicated bundle of contradictions. There were so many facets to her that I found it difficult to reconcile all her different characteristics and to put together the complete jigsaw that was Nana Ballyduane. It defied logic – or at least my logic – that this woman, whom I considered strong-willed and domineering and who did not suffer fools gladly, had married into an old farming household where living here before her were a mother-in-law, father-in-law and a brother-in-law, who later married and had two children before acquiring his own place. And to my astonishment, all of these in-laws credited her with being the peace-maker and facilitator, who caused all this complicated beehive of family relationships to work. It probably helped greatly that she was a capable and resourceful woman, who had, as a result of her upbringing, mastered the art of using everything that was available to good effect. She kept chickens, ducks and pigs to maintain a well-stocked kitchen cupboard, and was the creator of ample and good-quality fare for her extended family. Then, when one of her husband's nephews was left without parents as a result of a death in the family, she took him in too and treated him as one of her own. She was a woman of action not words, which meant that though she might not flatter you with compliments, if you hit a hard rock in life she came to your rescue, which caused one family member to say of her that she 'could kill you and cure you'. To all of the extended family she was known as 'The Missus', but to me she was Nana Ballyduane, and I sometimes wonder if she was a collection of many different women rolled into one.

In Nana's time large families were the order of the day but she had just three children, which was pretty minimalist for the times that were in it, and which she attributed to the fact that when she got married her child-bearing years were limited. Maybe her maturity on joining this long-tailed family was a contributory factor to her ability to ride the complex waves of family-in-law complications. Despite the fact that she was a woman of strongly held beliefs, she somehow managed to be flexible enough to manoeuvre through the deep waters of any internal family strife.

She had other strife to contend with too. This year, 2022, we remember the events that led to the internal conflicts of Irish politics which caused the Civil War and learn that on that historic night when voting on Treaty acceptance or rejection, the seven women who were in the Dáil voted against it. Recently, watching the reenactment of that night on TV brought memories of Nana Ballyduane flooding back to me and with them the realisation that she too would have stood with those women and voted against the Treaty. She was very political and had lived through the War of Independence, and would not have settled for less than going the whole hog. Years later, as she sat by her fire and read about the Northern Ireland leaders Edward Carson, William Craig and later Lord Basil Brookeborough, you could almost see the smoke coming out of her ears. Like the women of the French Revolution, she would, if given half a chance, have crawled on her hands and knees to the Border and cut the heads off all of them!

In the midst of the struggles that had preceded the Civil War, hers was a safe house for young IRA men on the run, and she was often raided at night by the British military and, later, the Black and Tans, an auxiliary force renowned for their lawlessness, unpredictability and cruelty. She refused to be intimated by any of them, and during one night-time raid when one of the British officers told her she reminded him of his mother was heard to inform him that his mother could not be up to much to rear a blackguard like him! And once the British were gone out of Ireland she would settle for no compromise other than complete riddance – and so was totally anti-Treaty.

When one of her two daughters (my mother) went on to marry someone who would have voted *for* the Treaty she must have wondered where she had gone wrong. In our house whenever she came to visit it was a case of 'Don't mention the war'. Unlike Nana Ballyduane, my mother, her daughter, was easygoing, gentle and patient, and believed that everyone was as good as they could be – a philosophy that neither her mother nor her husband espoused.

But in later years, despite Nana's armour-like exterior,

every once in a while she would decide that enough was enough, and take to her bed. She had made up her mind to call it a day. She would summon the local doctor and priest to attend her and both would dutifully arrive, knowing full well that there was actually nothing at all the matter with her. But they were smart enough to keep their opinions to themselves and humour her. On one such occasion I happened to be on holiday with her when this health crisis was in progress and I simply loved all the excitement that it engendered. Getting what was called the 'priest's table' ready was, for me, like preparing a stage for the high drama about to unfold. The doctor's coming, by comparison, caused no such excitement as he brought all his requirements in his brown leather bag. The only difference he brought into the house was his medical whiff that gave the kitchen and her bedroom a strange new aroma. Even after his departure, you could still smell his disinfecting presence around the house. But there was nothing else that was tangible about the doctor's visit with which I could become involved. The priest, however, was a totally different matter, and his requirements, as far as I was concerned, had endless possibilities as he was about to raise Nana from the dead! He was going to perform a miracle and I was determined that I was going to be a bedside witness to this resurrection.

A little wicker table that was usually tucked away in a corner of the room was cleared of clutter and brought centre-stage beside her bed, and draped with a lovely lace-edged, white tablecloth. This, to me, was the beginning of Great Things about to unfold. It was almost as good as decorating the annual May altar at home, which I loved. A crucifix and holy water were brought into action, and I was all for bringing along a retinue of Nana's statues from around the room, but these were dismissed by my mother, who had been called to arms despite probably also knowing full well that all this was probably much ado about nothing. Then came the highlight! A tall brass candlestick was taken down off the mantelpiece and after a quick polish, a blessed wax candle, preserved since the previous parish Mission, was unearthed out of a deep drawer in the sideboard and mounted on the candlestick. I desperately wanted to light the tall, yellowing candle, as to me its glow was indicative of the altar rituals at Mass on Sunday, which fascinated me. But my mother dismissed this and put me on point duty by the front door to watch out for the priest's car coming up the boreen, which would be her signal to light the candle prior to his arrival into the room. So this kept me occupied and out of her hair as I remained on standby. As soon as I heard the purr of the engine I shot up into the bedroom to announce his forthcoming arrival. I wanted to be in close proximity to witness all the actions first-hand.

But much to my disappointment, when he was eventually ushered into her room with a swirl of his black cassock, I was unceremoniously ushered out, missing all the excitement that I felt sure was about to unfold. I stood outside the firmly closed door with my ear cocked, but all I could catch was an inaudible murmur. I then had a belated regret that maybe I should have hidden under the bed from where I would have heard everything! But I instantly dismissed this belated temptation as the consequence of such deviousness were too dire to contemplate – if I was discovered under her bed it could be me instead of Nana facing my final end.

Two days later, instead of taking her final exit Nana was back in her chair by the fire and my temporary reprieve was over; her temporary lapse of interest in the running of the house, the farm and the country was forgotten. Over the years, she never lost her abiding interest in politics – global, national and local – and every day, even up to the day before she died, she spent hours reading the newspaper. She was well informed and loved to discuss the state of the nation with her many callers, and it certainly eased the flow of discussion if they shared her political views that over the years never changed.

# Chapter Three

# The Nana Knickers

O scar Wilde told us that we would all in time turn into our mothers and now when I look into the mirror and see my mother looking back out at me I'm inclined to agree with him. But he never told us that we might also, with the passage of more time, eventually turn into our grandmothers! This morning, when I donned my first Nana knickers, I knew that I was heading down that road. But sub-zero temperatures quickly eradicate the desire to look trendy, which is quickly replaced by an over-riding need to keep warm and comfortable. So, on went the Nana knickers!

As soon as I caught sight of myself in the merciless glare of the full-length bedroom mirror, strategically placed for critical appraisal before leaving the confines of the bedroom where anything is permissible, I came to a standstill. It was a moment of sharp realisation! I was transported back to my Nana's bedroom, remembering her nightly unrobing. Our generation hurriedly dress and undress, but our Nana's generation unrobed at their leisure. With the donning of the Nana knickers, I think I have joined the unrobing brigade. With my grandmother, this was an impressive nightly ritual and some nights I was her one child audience.

Her six-foot-tall frame had never tilted forward with the passage of years, so the removal of her layers was akin to the unrobing of a Charles de Gaulle or an Eamon de Valera, both of whom she resembled in stature, and revered. First off came her head gear, a knitted bonnet known to us children as a 'pixie', which was one of the favoured forms of female headgear of the time, knitted to the shape of the head, with two strings knotted together under the chin keeping it firmly in position. If made of cloth, these were called bonnets, but if knitted they were pixies, maybe because they resembled the head apparel supposedly worn by the pixies of the fairy world – in which there was a strong belief at that time. These wool pixies could be knitted in many colours, but our Nana's was always black, and she removed it only when she was preparing for bed and about to disappear from public life. Around the house or yard, or sitting on her chair by the fire, it never left her head. At bedtime, after carefully unknotting the two strings beneath her chin, the pixie got transferred from Nana's head to the brass head of the bedpost, where at first it did a bit of a twirling dance before settling around the bedhead, with its two strings dangling down along the black leg of the bed. Next off came the black cape that she wore around her shoulders, which was double-layered with scalloped edging, and was either knitted or crocheted, and was quite substantial and warm. When unclasped, this cape was swung onto the back of her leather-seated bedside armchair. Then she reached behind her back and undid the strings of her long, black apron, that was then eased off and folded carefully across the seat of the chair. All this was done slowly and with great precision and deliberation.

Then she walked over to the window that looked out over the farmyard and the fields of the farm. As she did this, she began to ease open the buttons down the front of her black satin blouse. There were two rows of tiny satin-covered buttons to be opened, and she took her time as her knowing fingers moved slowly from one button to the next, feeling her way down along as she looked out the window across the fields, commenting on the condition of the countryside and determining by the appearance of the night sky the forecast for the following day. Sometimes the size and shape of the moon came in for comment as she believed the nightly journey of the moon across the sky, as well as influencing the weather, also had a bearing on our collective state of mental stability.

If she had not already done so, she then took a break from the unrobing to wind her weights-and-chains clock that hung on the wall between the bedroom door and the large fireplace. Just beside the clock was a little cupboard set deep into the wide wall, which was her medicine chest where she kept a proliferation of herbal cures in evil-looking little black or green bottles. Amongst them was a poisonous-looking concoction knows as 'cascara'. To me it looked guaranteed to kill, but to Nana it was the elixir of life – indeed, she may have been right as it is actually regarded as having colon-cleansing properties. As she pulled down the chains of the clock they made a whirring sound as the weights climbed upwards, guaranteeing that the brass pendulum would continue to rhythmically swing back and forth to her satisfaction. Then she returned to her window-viewing and eased off her blouse, and this joined the shawl on the back of the chair. She then undid the waist of her long, black skirt that slid to the floor, and she stepped out of it. Then she picked up the skirt and carefully folded its pleats, arranging them across the chair-seat over her apron. Now she stood resplendent in her long-sleeved flowing white chemise and brilliant flaming-red petticoat. Sometimes this petticoat might be grey, and when the grey turn came around it was a big, drab disappointment for me. To me the appearance of that red petticoat was the high point of the unveiling. It seemed such a shame to have it submerged under all those drab black layers, but to Nana it was its warmth and usefulness that was of importance not its flamboyant appearance. Then the petticoat slid in folds down around her ankles and she stepped out of it – and this too joined the skirt on the seat of the chair.

Now the Nana knickers came into view. These varied in

colour from navy to blue to pink. But it was not the colour alone that made it impressive, but its voluptuous capacity. It stretched from beneath Nana's bosom continuing downwards in a flowing flounce to be whipped into an elasticated edge just above her knees. She eased up the gathered elasticated edge at each knee and snapped open the suspenders of her whalebone corset, three suspenders for each leg, two to the back and one to the front. Then she eased down one side of her knickers and snapped open the corset hooks down along that side and each one clicked loudly as it popped open. There was a harmonious rhythm to this clicking and I tried desperately every night to count and time the final click to coincide with the grand finale when she whipped off the whalebone corset. Then the corset lashed in a final crashing crescendo of bone and steel against the iron leg of the bed and it landed with an indefinable swirl of its many parts on top of the red petticoat. As far as I was concerned this was the grand finale! Corsets, though admittedly a more modified version, were still part of the female wardrobe up to the 1960s, even on the farm!

Then she sat on the side of the bed and slowly unlaced her high black boots which she placed underneath the chair, and then she rolled down her long, black woollen stockings. After this, her chemise was eased up over her head and a yellow bodice came into view. The final unveiling was hidden from my eyes as she then disappeared behind the large wardrobe and when she reappeared she was immersed in a long white nightdress, and her hair was released from the tight, restricting confines of her gigantic hairpins and cascaded down around her shoulders. She was transformed from my rigid, regal, forbidding grandmother into a slender, waif-like figure. Next she peeled the bedclothes back at her side of the bed and slowly eased herself on board and settled down into her feather tick, and then leaned back to be propped up in a hillside of feather pillows. Even though we were in the same bed we were on different plateaus as she was perched high above me on her mountain of pillows.

Then began the serious business of our night-prayer ritual. First the four evangelists were called into action:

Matthew, Mark, Luke and John
Bless the bed that I lie on
And if I die before I wake
The Lord I give my soul to take.

Having put the four evangelists on standby duty for the night it was time to visit Nazareth and see how Our Lady and the Holy Family were doing, and this was no short courtesy call. After each decade of the rosary Nana had a long list of invocations specific to each decade. But to me her rosary was a soothing mantra at the end of a long day and gradually I found myself being lulled into sleep by the continuous, repetitive prayers. But Nana was having none of falling asleep on the job and when she sensed from my voice that I was nodding off I got a sharp dig in the ribs and was abruptly brought back to reality.

The Nana

When the rosary came to an end, Nana was not yet finished and she then began to teach me a variety of prayers,
including a long, meandering prayer to my Guardian Angel.
That Guardian Angel prayer took weeks to get anchored
into my brain, but Nana was determined that this prayer was
going to stay with me forever.

Dear Angel ever at my side
How loving thou must be
To leave thy home in heaven above
And guard a sinful child like me
Thy beautiful and shining face
I see not thou so near
The sweetness of thy soft sweet voice
I am too deaf to hear
I cannot feel thee touch my hand
With pressure light and mild
To check me as my mother did
when I was but a child
But I have felt thee in my thoughts
Fighting against sin for me
And when my heart loves God
I know the sweetness is from thee
And when dear spirit I kneel down
Morning and night to pray
Something there is within my thoughts
To tell me thou art there
And when I pray thou prayest too

The prayer is all for me
But when I sleep thou sleepest not
But watcheth patiently.

It took a while, but finally I got it! And the amazing thing is that now, even after all these years, I can still remember it. So Nanas can leave long-lasting prints on the minds of their grandchildren.

Chapter Four

# Now and Then

One of the blessings of grandchildren is that they snap open memory doors in your mind and take you back into long-forgotten scenes from your own childhood. This happened to me recently and proved to be a very joyful experience.

Every Thursday evening I take my granddaughter, nine-year-old Ellie, to ballet. Now, it was far from ballet that I was reared! But from an early age I have always been intrigued by that world because by some strange chance of fate a magazine with pictures of Margot Fonteyn pirouetting across a page had found its way into our remote farmhouse at a time when we were trudging to school through muddy fields in heavy, laced-up, strong leather boots. This magazine was probably brought home by a returning emigrant or might indeed have been purchased by myself with hard-earned potato-picking money in our local news agency at a time when I was big into film stars and the royals.

That picture of the then-famous Margot, whirling her body into unbelievable poses, led to a barefooted me in my long, woolly nightdress endeavouring to imitate her whirling activities across a draughty bedroom floor and tip my quivering big toe against the high black rail of our iron bedhead. Back then, I thought that as a result of mastering this flexibility I would walk like a queen. But in today's world, ballet for children has moved into far more accessible terrain and in our parish hall a young local woman, 'Miss Sarah', as the children call her, leads them into all kinds of elegant, quivering poses.

Walking to and from ballet with Ellie affords us the opportunity to have long chats about all kinds of everything. One Thursday evening just before Christmas she was overflowing with anticipatory enthusiasm. As we approached the village corner where every year before Christmas we erect a large tree, her exuberance for the upcoming Christmas simply flowed over. She danced around the area where the tree would soon stand, pouring forth a waterfall of non-stop questions:

'Nana, when is our big village Christmas tree going up?'

'Nana, when are you getting your tree?'

'Nana, are you coming with us to get our tree?'

'Nana, when is the big crib going up in front of the church?'

When she finally stopped to draw breath I tried to

slot in some answers. Her overflowing enthusiasm for the approaching Christmas was contagious and brought to mind the observation of a wise friend: 'The old should surround themselves with the young.' Ellie's exuberance was energising.

The following morning as I slowly emerged from the depths of a deep sleep into a semi-conscious wakefulness, I was still cloaked in Ellie's Christmas enthusiasm. Do you ever find that in those early morning moments between sleep and full wakefulness that you are in a pool of other-mindedness into which mysterious things may float? And into my mind this morning floated a long-forgotten image of two wooden toy horses, one green and one red. On a long-ago Christmas Eve, when I was about six years old, I got a present of two little hand-carved wooden horses. One was red and the other green. At the time, exchanging gifts at Christmas was not common practice, so this was a totally unexpected gift and may have been motivated by the fact that my little brother, aged four, had died that November – and maybe this kind-hearted neighbour hoped that these two little horses might bring some healing and comfort that Christmas. This neighbour was my godmother and whether she got her brother to carve the two little horses or got a handier neighbour to carve and paint them I have no idea, but for me that Christmas they provided hours of comforting play, and now, years later, I look back with appreciation and gratitude at the depth of kindness that motivated those warm-hearted, generous neighbours to do what they did.

At that time, horses were very much part of our farming world, so my two little wooden horses were immediately christened Paddy and James after our two working horses, and took me out into the fields where, under my direction, they ploughed the fields and mowed the hay and provided hours of endless pleasure.

Ellie's happy Christmas chattering had awakened the memory of that long-forgotten kindness. So the next morning as I again lay in bed half-awake I decided to take time out to journey back down a memory road to discover if there were other locked doors into forgotten kindnesses. And so back came the memory of Katie Mark.

Along the road between our house and our Nana's lived Katie, who was of the Nana generation. She was known as Katie Mark, maybe because her husband's name was Mark, and they had one son known as Johnny Mark, about whom his mother constantly worried because he was in the American air force. She was worried that he could be shot down by enemy aircraft. So she had all us neighbouring children praying for 'the safe return of Johnny Mark'.

On the way back to Nana's house I loved to visit Katie because she was gentle and kind, and to me was what I thought a *real* Nana should be! My Nana was not in the least bit like Katie Mark. After a little while chatting, Katie always checked if I was praying for Johnny Mark. Most nights I did kneel by my bed and say three Hail Marys for 'the safe return of Johnny Mark', though some nights I forgot.

But then Katie showed me a kindness that committed

me to total dedication to praying for her far-away son. Her house was an Aladdin's cave of intriguing bits and pieces, and in many ways was a reflection of herself. She did not dress in the customary long black garb of Nana Ballyduane, but in whites, creams and pale greys, with her white hair caught up in a loose knot on top of her head from which it constantly escaped and curled down around her face like an unruly hedge. Our Nana wore her hair in a similar fashion, but her topknot was firmly held in place by a circle of gigantic, aggressive hairpins, so it did not have any chance of escape. Our Nana, and indeed other Nanas, referred to this hair arrangement as the 'kuck', which was probably a vague translation from the Gaelic *cnoc* (hill), which indeed it did resemble. But Katie's hair arrangement was more like a bunch of tangled bushes that somehow was totally in keeping with her personality.

Amongst Katie's bits and pieces were many fascinating items probably brought back from all over the world by her son and also her husband, who, for some strange reason, worked in America, which was totally intriguing and mysterious to us children because at that time going to America was like going to the moon. But everything about Katie was unusual and her house had an air of mystery, overflowing with intriguing nick-nacks, and as I sat by Katie's fire my eyes kept wandering around the room to all her little bits and pieces. There was one particular piece that was always a magnet to my gaze. Perched on a shelf above the kitchen window was a miniature doll's dresser. It was perfectly made, with tiny brass hooks for little cups along the front of the shelves and beneath the lap of the dresser were two tiny doors with brass knobs. When I visited Katie, my eyes were always drawn to this little dresser and though I never touched it, I played with it in my imagination.

When you dropped in on Katie, whether you were child or adult, she offered you tea, coffee or cocoa. Her cocoa was the best you ever tasted – steaming hot, rich brown, with creamy froth and saturated with sugar. One evening, while I was savouring this gorgeous beverage, Katie reached up and took down the doll's dresser from the high shelf. I held my breath, thinking that I was at long last going to be allowed play with it. But something much better was about to happen! She handed me the little dresser and told me that it was mine to take home with me. I was flooded with appreciation and speechless with delight, and every night from then on before getting into bed I was on my knees praying for the safe return of Johnny Mark!

As Katie did not have a daughter or a granddaughter, the chances were that the little doll's dresser, which she obviously treasured as was shown by its location in her kitchen, probably came from her own childhood. It was an incredible act of kindness on her part to give it to me. Her kindness reached across the generation gap that separated us and was never forgotten.

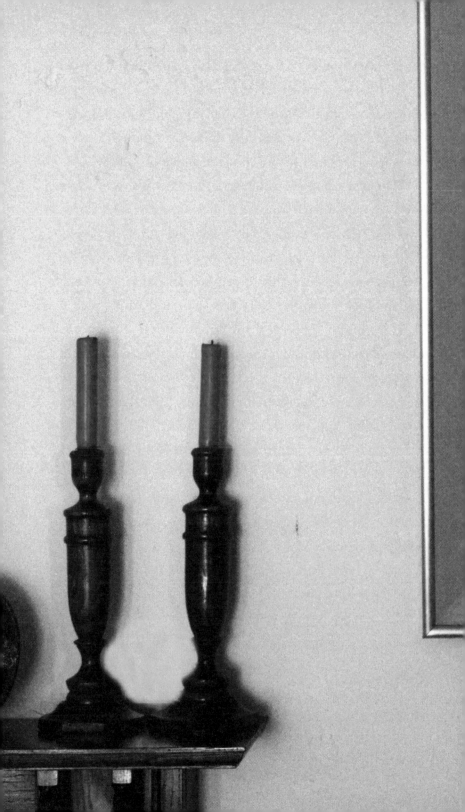

*My parents' wedding photo.*

Enamel utensils and carbolic soap were much in use.

**Above:** *Our home farmhouse, which was typical of its time.*
**Opposite:** *My mother in her Nana days.*

*Rosary beads were in constant use for the nightly recital, and at wakes and funerals.*

The butter churn was used to
churn cream into butter, and there
was one in most farmhouses where
homemade butter was the norm.

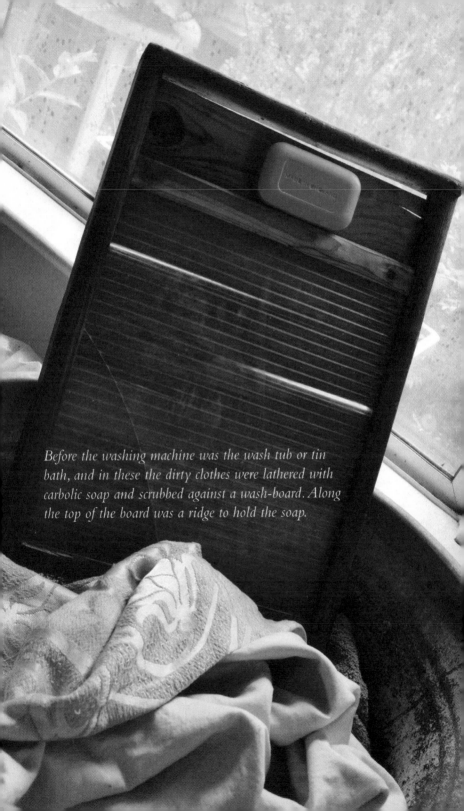

Before the washing machine was the wash tub or tin bath, and in these the dirty clothes were lathered with carbolic soap and scrubbed against a wash-board. Along the top of the board was a ridge to hold the soap.

*These large teapots came into action for the Stations, the threshing and family gatherings. One such teapot might be shared between several houses.*

Chapter Five

# Thank Heaven for Little Girls

When my mother decided to get married she simply walked a few miles east the road and turned in the gate of the Taylor homestead where she continued the open-door policy of both Grandmother Taylor and Nana Ballyduane. Down through the years, generations of young people from our region had boarded the *Innisfallen* ship for England or the liners in Cobh to find their way to the four corners of the world, resulting, years later, in a constant streams of emigrants and their descendants returning to the home place. As was the family tradition, they were afforded a warm welcome and my mother was as welcoming to her Taylor in-law visitors as she was to her own O'Keeffes. As a matter of fact, she was far better informed on the Taylor family tree than was my father. And when she became the mother of five daughters, my mother had her own catering team, which sometimes caused my father to roll his eyes to heaven and proclaim, 'Pity the man who has five daughters!' When his first daughter to get married produced a further three daughters he accepted ruefully that he was indeed living under a 'Petticoat Government'. These three new grandchildren lived in the nearby town and were constant visitors to the home farm at Lisdangan, and to them my mother became Nana Taylor.

As a grandmother, my mother was a total contrast to Nana Ballyduane, and my mother's grandchildren adored her. As the first grandchildren, Mary, Eileen and Treasa became part and parcel of life in our house. They considered themselves to be part of us and of the country, though they lived in the nearby town. Their sense of belonging was nurtured by all who then lived on the home farm to which they made twice-weekly visits, every Friday night and Sunday afternoon. They also spent their entire summer holidays with their Nana and Grandad, whom they called Dee probably because his name was Denis, and Dee was as good as they could manage. The youngest granddaughter, Treasa, now a young grandmother herself, says that a warm inner glow graduating to a smile is what she feels when she recalls Nana Taylor, and her very first memories are of holidaying on the farm with her Nana whom she remembers as a gentle, warm and calm person.

On Friday nights they would rush from the car in the front door and head for the back kitchen where Nana would have freshly baked currant bread at the ready. It was the only time that Treasa can remember her Nana telling them to go easy as she believed that fresh bread was bad for them. But that did not deter them from eating big wedges of her lovely, warm bread.

They then spent the entire evening rooting through the drawers of the kitchen dresser. To them these drawers were full of interesting and fascinating bits and pieces – old letters, battered copies of *The Messenger*, bottle corks, bits of string, old sketch pads probably used by us when we were small, and spare buttons. They then proceeded to empty the contents of the drawers onto the kitchen table and rearrange all these different bits and pieces in a new order, only to return the following week and repeat the same job all over again. Their sorting out of those two drawers was a case of history repeating itself because it was something that we too had done as children. It is difficult in today's world to explain the fascination that those two drawers held for children, but they somehow had the magic of an Aladdin's cave. My grandchildren now have a playroom full of toys, but those two drawers were our playroom. Even later, as an adult, when I came back home I still went through those drawers feeling that in some way they were the pulse of the house and told the story of what had happened while I was away.

I found it intriguing that for the next generation those drawers were equally interesting, and, of course, their Nana left them at it, pleased to have them so happily occupied. She was a woman of immense patience and they can never remember her getting cross with them. When spring came her three little granddaughters would make a beeline for the room off the back kitchen and peer in at the day-old chicks under the heat lamp. They were fascinated by the chirping and movement of these little birds. Indeed, we too as children had been filled with excitement on the day we came home from school to find these little chicks in residence. They had arrived in long, strong cardboard boxes with round perforated holes for air circulation. Like Mary, Eileen and Treasa, we too were allowed to shake the chicken mash to feed the chicks in the run that was set up around the heating lamp. Providing the chicks with water was a bit more complicated as this meant pouring water into a jampot and then placing a saucer on top of the pot and turning the whole menagerie upside down, so the water would seep out slowly into the saucer. From this saucer the chicks could then safely sip, but this manoeuvre with the jampot and saucer required a certain amount of dexterity not always achievable by small girls anxious to help, and could sometimes finish up in an unplanned waterfall. But eventually we all got the hang of it.

After a few weeks the chicks grew bigger and were moved to an outside henhouse. This henhouse was located near the barn and when on holiday Mary, Eileen and Treasa trooped up there daily to collect the eggs – but, unlike us who were quite used to the hens, they were not so brave when it came to the henhouse because the hens would jump around and there were strange smells that did not appeal to them, whereas to us this was all part of daily life. But their Nana acted as mediator, encouraging them to feel at ease with her growing birds. She had a great interest in her hens, and she reared geese and ducks as well. My father had no patience in dealing with fowl so this job was left totally to my mother who treated all her birds with care and compassion.

Holidays on the farm were part of the childhood of these first grandchildren. They loved sleeping in the middle room upstairs, enveloped in a deep, soft feather tick. This room was over the kitchen, so was lovely and cosy. There they were lulled to sleep by the distant hum of voices from the kitchen below. But if the volume rose in the kitchen or there was a sudden burst of laughter, they jumped out of bed to investigate and ran half-way down the stairs where they sat on their viewing step. From that step they had a secret vantage point. Years previously we too had used that little viewing point. There was a hole in a knot of wood which we could peep through and get a full view of what was happening in the kitchen. Three steps further down, hanging on the wall at the turn of the stairs leading into the kitchen was a copy of the Easter Proclamation, of which Nana Ballyduane would have greatly approved – and even though the War of Independence was in the past this Proclamation was part of our history.

Over the years my mother ran an open house where relations and neighbours, sure of a warm welcome, were constantly calling. From their observation point on the stairs, the little girls noticed that one local man who came every night 'roving' – visiting his neighbours – sometimes had a little too much to drink and they watched with intense interest from the distance of their vantage point on the stairs while their Nana fed him to sober him up. They felt that in this, as in every situation, their Nana's sense of understanding and kindness was ever-present.

They loved the summertime and saving the hay, which meant a busy time in the kitchen for all of them. The men doing the work had their dinner in the middle of the day and in the afternoon the girls headed with Nana to the meadow with an enamel bucket full of milky tea and plates of freshly made apple tart. They would all sit on cocks of hay around the big central wynd of hay and drink the warm, sugary tea with the workers. This was a chance to relax and have fun, and for them to get to know and chat to the neighbouring farmers who were helping. Weeks later these wyndes of hay were loaded onto the float and drawn home by one of the farm horses. The girls lined up in the barn to go to the meadow for spins on the float and once the wynd of hay was secure on the float in the meadow the girls would make space for themselves behind it and settle down, with feet trailing above the ground, for a bumpy spin back through the fields to the barn. This was the experience that we too had as children and it was lovely to see the girls getting the same enjoyment from it.

They knew that her religious belief was an important part of their Nana's life and when they stayed with her the rosary was said every night. The kitchen chairs were pulled out from the table so that everyone could lean on one while kneeling on the floor. When their Grandad threw his cap on the floor the rosary began. Their Nana had a long list of prayers after every decade, and she finished off with the saying of the 'Hail Holy Queen' prayer. But what is most memorable for them now are her 'trimmings' of the rosary. She had a list of people she prayed for and she called on many saints for assistance. The children's answering job, led by their Grandad, was to chant back in response to each saint's name: 'Pray for us.' If extra pressure needed to be applied on heavenly bodies to answer a special need, Nana lit a candle at the centre of the parlour table. Her favourite prayer that she taught them was the '*Memorare*', and it is a prayer that they still say when life is testing their mettle, and they always think of her when saying it.

On Sundays they always went to Mass in the nearby town where they lived with their mother and father and sat with their parents in the main aisle of the parish church, but as soon as Mass was over they ran across to the side aisle where Nana was sitting. After Mass, Nana was in no hurry to leave the church and, as instructed by their mother, they sat quietly with her while she finished her prayers. She was good to pray and often her daughters living far from home and many of her friends would write asking for prayers on stressful occasions and requesting her to light a candle, which she always did. The children sometimes helped her to light candles on the church candelabra, and then they accompanied her out of the church and walked across the churchyard with her where she stopped at a wooden hut to buy *The Irish Catholic* and *The Messenger*, and they knew that she often sent money to help the missions who appealed for assistance in these publications.

When going to mass in winter Nana wore ankle boots and if going on a special visit she always wore a tweed suit and a very stylish hat. At home her uniform was a cross-over dark blue or light blue overall, which was comfortable and practical. She had a great love of gardening which she passed on to her grandchildren. She enjoyed planting seeds, especially sweet peas and nasturtiums, and was very keen on taking slips and planting them into pots – and now these grandchildren do the same and exchange slips between each other's gardens. They associate Nana Taylor with geraniums as she always had them on her parlour window, and in her garden she had a huge hydrangea, so now both plants bring back memories of her.

As she got older she never complained about her ailments and was far more interested in what they were doing, and this left a sense of her loving warmth and caring in their lives.

## Chapter Six

# Ireland's Call

My sister Mary was in one of the shoals of Irish emigrants who sailed out of Cork harbour to England in the 1950s where she eventually settled in Kent and became more English than the English themselves. Once while on holiday with her I found myself part of a posh garden lunch which she and her Welsh husband were hosting as a fund-raiser for the Conservative Party in the leafy lanes of Pluckley. Nana Ballyduane must surely have been turning in her grave! But all was not lost! When Ireland and Wales clashed in a rugby final, a supremacy battle brewed in their house. Her husband's Welsh blood ignited, but, ignoring the rise in temperature, my sister sat at a distance from him and the rest of the family pretending to be absorbed in a garden magazine. But she was fooling no one – when Ireland scored she beamed triumphantly at no one in particular and if Ireland won she rose from her chair humming 'Ireland's Call' and strode past her family out into the garden. With the sporting challenge she had reverted to type. Nana Ballyduane was waving the green flag.

Her daughter, Lisa, visited both her Welsh and Irish grand-mothers on a regular basis and these women had two very different lifestyles and completely different personalities. It was interesting to hear the stories of how these two grand-mothers influenced her life. Lisa called her Welsh grand-mother 'Grandma' and her Irish grandmother 'Nana'. And, with that in mind, one wonders what's in a name?

Grandma in Wales lived in a trim bungalow on the edge of Welshpool on the Welsh border. At the front of her house was a carefully tended lawn with a moulded stone edging along the path leading to a scrubbed, mosaic front-door step. At the back was a walled garden with beds and rocker-ies of bright, well-maintained flowers. Just like her house, Grandma in Wales presented a face of ordered respectability to the world. As a child, Lisa felt that a visit to Grandma was an exercise in 'good behaviour'. Her mother hinted to Lisa that no one had been quite good enough for Grandma's only child, who had graduated from Cambridge with top-class honours, and Grandma was very much into keeping up standards. So her grandchildren were left in no doubt that when visiting Grandma they had to behave impeccably. Nevertheless, Grandma still had her pluses as she always had lucozade in her fridge, an unheard of treat in those days unless you were ill. On one visit she presented Lisa and her brother with two matching cowboy outfits and, as a confirmed tomboy, Lisa loved her for not making the usual mistake of buying her some girly toy. Full marks!

Once a day, Grandma would take her on a walk downtown to a tobacconist/sweet shop she owned. They would call in to see Mrs Thomas who looked after it for her. This visit should have been an exciting prospect for a child – a Grandma with a sweet shop! But Lisa recalls no such excitement. She latched on very early to the knowledge that she was not destined to get any of those sweets. But the trip did have one benefit: the routine was the same each day – call into the sweet shop, then into a grocer's to buy a small pot of yoghurt and a pot of ice cream. After tea Grandma ate the yogurt and Lisa was given the pot of ice cream. Grandma told her that she could not have the yogurt because of all the bugs in it, but Lisa was delighted to have a pot of ice cream all to herself, which would be unheard of at home.

When Lisa was nine Grandma moved in with them due to ill health and to accommodate this they moved into a much larger house. But a few weeks later Grandma died. Lisa knew that when important people died it was announced on the Six o'clock News on the BBC. So she was a bit perplexed when her Grandma's death did not get a mention.

Lisa's visits to Nana in Ireland were a different story. While Wales had many rules and behavioural limitations, trips to Nana in Ireland had none. Once they had arrived in Ireland they went to stay first with one of their many aunts where they would meet up with all the cousins – and there were a lot of them! They were thrilled because being part of a nuclear family in England consisted of parents and a sibling or two, but in Ireland they found themselves part of a family of countless children. Not only that, but in England a cousin was a strictly defined entity – your mother or father's sibling's offspring, no more no less. In Ireland that definition did not seem to apply and instead produced a huge crop of 'relatives'. Lisa found that a 'cousin' encompassed not only the close blood relatives, but many remoter offspring who had some tenuous family links. One summer, on arriving in their mother's home town, they called to the children's playground where Lisa's nine-year-old brother managed to pick a fight with some little lad – who turned out to be a 'cousin'! So all was instantly forgiven!

The absolute highlight of the trip to Ireland was the long stay with Nana. She lived on a farm, of course, which provided endless delights and wonderful avenues of exploration. Their mother had told them many exciting tales of growing up there, and this made them love the very idea of the place. Getting to Nana's involved driving down a long track with several gates that they were dispatched out of the car to open and close. The last gate led past the milking parlour and if they were lucky enough to arrive at milking time their uncle would emerge in his overalls to welcome them. For the first few days Lisa hardly understood one word he said until her ear grew accustomed to the Cork accent. But she felt his warm welcome and did not need words.

Then it was down to the old, pink-rendered farmhouse,

their mother's home place which had an aura of timelessness about it. Out on the doorstep stood Nana, wearing a blue housecoat of uncertain vintage and smelling of a mixture of soda bread and turf. Then came the joy of a warm hug from her. Seeing relatives after long gaps between visits can sometimes cause uncertainty for children, but not so with Nana. She had a warm smile and a calmness about her which told you that not much was going to bother her. You knew instinctively that she was kind – and that she would have a relaxed attitude to any misdemeanours that you could dream up!

At Nana's there didn't seem to be too much that was forbidden. At home in England they lived in a modern housing estate where supervisory neighbours kept an eye on children's behaviour and the entertainment choices were reliant on bought toys or trips to parks. Compared to that, the variety and wildness of a farm was thrilling. Behind the farmhouse was an ancient fort protected by dense woods, and they had the run of it. Plus, there was a stream that ran near the house which was perfect for dams. Further afield was a river that ran through the farm, and was far away from adults and supervision. In that river they had great fun fishing for collies (tiny minnows). Occasionally their Granddad came to do some proper fishing, and they loved the trout that he caught and that Nana cooked on a warm summer's evening.

Nana would appear in the kitchen early each morning with a saucepan of porridge, and with cream and brown sugar. Then she would produce strong tea and homemade, nutty brown bread and butter. The dinner, which was in the middle of the day, always seemed to be bacon, cabbage and potatoes in their skins, and supper was more brown bread and currant cake. During hay-making the children were busy all morning filling tins with brown bread and cake, then making tea to take out to the busy workers in the field.

Lisa loved collecting the hen eggs with Nana – a very different experience from popping into the shop in England. Nana would lead her through pens of inquisitive calves and barking dogs to get to the henhouse and then tutor her in carefully burrowing into the nest boxes to find the eggs beneath the straw and deposit them carefully in her basket. These were the best eggs Lisa ever tasted.

Their time in Ireland was always too short and all too soon they would be heading tearfully back home. As a small compensation they would often be richer due to various relatives quietly pressing large 'donations' into their hands, whispering, 'Buy yourself something nice.' This was a very common practice in Ireland at the time, and it often made children feel very special. Their father had very strict ideas about pocket money so to be handed what seemed like vast sums of money was very welcome. Nana was as prone to doling out presents as the rest of the family, but with her it was less predictable and a paper item pressed into your hand might equally well be a £10 note or a prayer to her favourite saint. Either way, Lisa thinks that she gave them what she thought they needed.

Nana's laid-back attitude meant that her living space

could sometimes become a bit chaotic. In her room she had a large press which seemed to contain every gift, card and family artefact that had ever come into her possession, and anyone visiting her was likely to leave with an unpredictable gift, which was another one of her random acts of generosity.

Lisa feels lucky to have known Nana in Ireland – my mother – for a good few years as she lived until Lisa was in her early twenties. As she grew older she appreciated her Nana's mellow attitude to life even more. Also, she was continually impressed by how many people her Nana knew. If Lisa met anyone while on holiday in Cork, Nana knew their parents, grandparents and cousins, and could tell their whole family history! Lisa found this amazing.

Lisa was always felt very close to her Nana in Ireland and admired her kindness and the fact that she only saw the best in her. In her later years Nana had a stroke and was ill for a while, and during one visit after her stroke she expressed one regret to Lisa and it was that she had never come to visit them.

One evening after her last visit Lisa was walking by the sea near her home in Wales and was suddenly touched by a very warm feeling of love and the sense that someone was near. That evening her mother rang to say that Nana had died. Lisa often wonders if Nana had finally made her visit across the water to say farewell ... She hopes so!

# Chapter Seven

# Nana in the House

One of our wise old neighbours used to regularly proclaim philosophically 'one woman–one kitchen'. This comment probably came from his observation of the family conflict that sometimes ensued when a daughter-in-law and mother-in-law had a clash of personalities when they had to share the one kitchen. It could be a situation strewn with endless potential for family friction and volcanic emotive eruptions. And because conflict is grist to the mill of writers it sometimes became a subject in Irish literature. It probably took the wisdom of Solomon and the patience of Job to effect a harmonious relationship in some circumstances, but when it was achieved the young couple had a round-the-clock babysitting service and the older couple the joy of their grandchildren. Maybe one of the secrets to its success was the provision of separate living quarters in advance, to prevent any turmoil from evolving.

Upstairs at the western end of our old farmhouse was a spare room which was a haven for my hoarding mother, and beneath it and connected by a wonky stairs was a room that my beekeeping brother had converted into his honey-extraction quarters. When he got married, these two rooms were converted into living quarters for my parents, which gave both couples breathing space and gave the grandchildren, when they arrived, the free run of both places.

Aileen was the youngest of my brother's family to grow up in the house where I was born. I found it intriguing when visiting to witness the changes the years had brought. She called my mother Granny Taylor in contrast to her other grandchildren who called her Nana Taylor. My mother was eighty when Aileen was born in 1975, and Aileen remembers her as a gentle lady full of peace and generosity, who, whenever the need arose, was her defender and advisor in the family circle. There were two years between Aileen and her brother Dominic, so that meant she got to spend two years home alone with the grownups, which she cherishes. Her Dad was out on the farm and her Mom busy cooking, baking and running the house, so this meant that every morning she'd ramble down to Granny and Granda, who lived in their own corner known as 'The Flat' at one end of the house.

To Aileen the Flat was her Montessori school. Here Granny and Granda taught her how to form her letters and numbers, and even more important practical skills, like how to tie her shoelaces and free-out the stem of Granda's pipe with pipe cleaners. Granda was often still in bed when Aileen would arrive, so she would climb in beside him and relish the heat and cuddles. Her Granda had a great love of nature and they would often peruse big, colourful books of exotic plants, birds and foreign places. Granny was more interested in good food and good-quality material for sewing. While Aileen and her Granda were travelling the jungles of the world, Nana would be tending to more practical matters like washing the ware or mending clothes, whilst still listening to the 'man of the moment' – second only to God himself – Gay Byrne. Aileen still remembers his lively introductory tune and Gay's eloquent tone – and Granny listening with such reverence. And Granda was often heard tut-tutting at the foolishness of folk. But her Granny's real area of expertise was teaching Aileen and her siblings their prayers, and to them she was very prayerful and holy.

As Aileen grew a bit older and better able to read and write, she became her Granny's personal assistant. She collected her pension, did her shopping and kept up her correspondence to family and friends all over the world. The Mill Hill Fathers were regular communicators and got a healthy financial contribution from Granny on a regular basis. She also graduated to being her Granny's hairdresser and chiropodist. But one job her Granny loved to do herself was to walk out around the yard to collect 'cippins' – little bits of branches that had fallen off trees – for the fire and go for walks around the fields. This, of course, kept her fit, and it always amazed Aileen that she could touch her toes with such ease even in her eighties.

On Sunday mornings Granny went to Mass with the family. She dressed in a blue coat in the summer and brown in the winter, and always wore a lovely silky scarf, carried a real leather handbag and wore suede ankle boots – or 'bootees' as she called them herself. Granny sat in the front of their Leyland Jeep and they all motored into town. In the church, Granny sat in the 'women's aisle' as it was then known, and Dominic and Aileen accompanied her. She made time for everyone she met. Aileen always sensed that she was a much-loved and respected woman in the parish. She greeted all in a friendly, sincere way and listened to them intently. She didn't crowd anyone with talk or monopolise the conversation, and Aileen remembers that she was a great listener. When Mass was over they lit candles and made their way down town to Granny's friend's shop, known as Lizzy May's. Here Aileen saw Nana really enjoy Lizzy May's company and they often laughed at days gone by when they had gone to school together. Lizzy May was a generous lady and would always give Granny's companion (Aileen herself) sweets – not the cheap ones either, but very nice ones or even sometimes a bar of chocolate. That was the best!

When it came to food, Granny was into quality control. She was a fount of knowledge in relation to seasoning and flavour. Special dishes, such as the Christmas stuffing, were always tested by Granny to determine if they needed extra flavouring. She was obsessed with the need for iron in the children's diet so she tried to sneak nettles into their cabbage when they were in season. Granny reckoned they wouldn't taste the nettles – but they begged to differ. She was a great teacher and often felt that they lacked patience and were rushing ahead too fast, and so she would often exclaim 'Hold your horses!' as she strove to slow them down, take stock, and review what they were too hurriedly trying to achieve. Often there would be arguments and rows amongst them, and Granny would always quote the same poem. Here's an extract:

Let dogs delight to bark and bite,
For God hath made them so;
Let bears and lions growl and fight,
For 'tis their nature to;
But, children, you should never let
Your angry passions rise;
Your little hands were never made
To tear each other's eyes.

This poem often served to calm the battle. Granny always wanted to keep the peace, and she was a great woman to run to when you came out the worst in a fracas. She'd calm things down, listen to what went wrong, offer her advice and maybe even give a treat to make it all better!

As Granny lived to the ripe age of ninety-four there was a constant stream of exiles coming to visit her, looking for long-lost roots and wanting to talk about times gone by.

She also had various people who had worked on the farm or in the house come back to visit her over the years and they all expressed their gratitude for the kindness she had shown them. She had wonderful respect for people and thought everyone was as good as they could be. This stuck with Aileen – she felt it was great advice for life and getting along with people. Cousins brought potential suitors for perusal and approval. Granny wouldn't be a harsh judge, but could bring attention to potential causes for concern. She was a sage advisor.

She never spoke ill of anyone or anything except the fox. Whenever Aileen thinks about her Granny, her loathing for the fox brings a little poem to mind:

A man may have a thousand friends
And not have one to spare
He may have just one enemy
But meets the fecker everywhere.

They'd all be sitting down watching a programme about wildlife on TV and, next thing, a fox would appear. Aileen's first reaction would be to remark on how cute the cubs were. But her Granny would become enraged. 'Look at that bloody devil!' she would declare, her face filling with annoyance. Aileen would protest, 'But, Granny, he is so beautiful.' Granny would have none of it! He had killed so many of her geese and chickens that he was beyond redemption. Even the cute little fox cubs playing merrily in the grass couldn't win Granny over. She could never forgive the fox. These appearances of the fox on TV were the only time that Aileen ever saw venom in Granny. Apart from that, that she was a calm and lovely lady, which led Aileen to conclude that we all have our triggers, even the best of us!

Granny was always the recipient of exciting post. At Christmas big, padded cards came from their Aunty Eileen in Canada and from others all around the world. Through-out the year, postcards and letters came from many interest-ing locations. As an avid stamp collector, Aileen benefited from this correspondence, although she did have competi-tion from the missions who could make money from these stamps. So she had to share her spoils.

Aileen remembers Granny's press was always full of lovely things – elegant scarves, sweet-smelling lotions and potions, and lovely, delicate ornaments and trinkets. She liked the good things in life. Granny always drank from a delicate, bone-china cup and saucer. She loved tea and Aileen believes that Granny's tea was like a hug from the inside out. In terms of treats, Granny had to have plenty of secret hiding places as sweet-toothed thieves were common raiders on her usual hiding spots. Her Marietta biscuits were rarely in demand, but were accepted as a last resort.

Aileen thinks now that her Granny was a wonderful person to have in her life, kind and generous and always there for them, or indeed anyone who needed her help, a very gentle and sincere person with great wisdom and a sense of what was important. Her greatest piece of advice,

Aileen now feels, was: 'People are as good as they can be', never criticising what they were or questioning their behaviour but simply accepting them as they were. She never judged or spoke ill of people and had a true Christian mind, and it came through in her words and in her actions. Aileen feels now that she was a wonderful example to her of how to live life.

# Chapter Eight

# Home to the Hills

At what point in your life do you stop referring to the house where you were born and grew up as 'home' and apply it to your later home? For years after coming to Innishannon I would still refer to going back to the home farm as 'going home'. My husband Gabriel used to smile and say, 'You're going back to the hills.' And he was right because after leaving Innishannon and then Macroom behind and going through the little village of Carriganimma there was a turn in the road where the landscape changed. Once you had rounded a specific corner the whole countryside stretched out in front of you with the hills rolling away as far as the eye could see. These were my hills and at that specific point I felt that I was on home ground where Mullaghanish mountain was the St Peter at my gate into heaven. My boys, too, loved going to the hills where their grandparents welcomed them with open arms. To them it was the wide open spaces of the farm that fired their imagination and one of them came back from one long summer holiday informing us that he had been on an African safari. At the end of the summer my mother came on holidays to Ballybunion with us for a week where she kept a watchful eye on her grandchildren in case they would venture too far into the sea. On arriving in Ballybunion, her first purchase after the usual shovels and spades were sailor hats, which she plonked on all their heads for easy traceability. This worked a treat as from her seat beside the beach she could keep an eye on the sailor hats that pin-pointed exactly where the children were. In the late afternoon they were all summoned to a little summer teahouse on the beach where she fed them lemonade and cream buns and fast-melting wafer ice cream. If at this stage, the tide was coming in and they began the challenging job of trying to block it with enormous sandcastles around which the obliging tide filled their moats, but eventually flattened their towering sandy blockades. From her ring-side seat Nana acted in an advisory engineering capacity.

But it was at night that their Nana and themselves really enjoyed each other's company in a big way when they all headed up town for the night life. But before leaving the guest house where we were staying there was a long session of balancing their financial affairs so that all participants were on an equal entertainment footing. Once their banking arrangements were to the satisfaction of all, they headed off in the direction of the blaring music that now poured from the 'Merries' halls along the street. Then the years seemed to peel off my mother. The boys took charge as they played bingo and one-armed bandits with her. She got as excited as they did when a one-armed bandit occasionally coughed up a flow of coins. When he did, it was time for her refereeing skills again so as to avoid a 'winner takes all' scenario. Everybody had to be kept happy in her book. As far as the boys were concerned, Nana had the final say in their financial world.

If Lady Luck did not smile on them Nana was always good to float a loan. They had hilarious times together. On these nights I seldom accompanied them feeling that this was their time with their beloved Nana when the age difference between them seemed to melt away and my mother became the girlish fun person that I had seldom seen. At the end of the night they pooled their resources to buy milk and fluffy biscuits to be eaten on the way home while sitting on a bench along the clifftop from where they could listen to the sea crashing off the rocks down below. When the weather turned stormy, Ballybunion could be a challenging place to hold your ground, especially if you were very small, and the littlest lad used to cling to his Nana's hand with the instruction, 'Nana, you hold my hand or the wind might blow me away.'

Years later the two of them laughed, remembering his request. By then that tide of years had turned and he was now her support system. They loved it when Nana came to stay in Innishannon where she took over in the kitchen and cooked all their favourite dishes, with tapioca and rice pudding heading the dessert list. If a row erupted between them, she trotted out the same calming verse that she had used years previously to calm our stormy waters:

Birds in their little nests agree;
And 'tis a shameful sight,
When children of one family
Fall out, and chide, and fight.

And it still worked because they were very conscious that Nana's wishes had to be respected no matter what pressing scores had to be levelled between themselves.

In my mother's declining years our only daughter was born and we called her Lena after her grandmother. Their Nana had enriched the boys' lives, and I was glad that the two Lenas had some years together during which she and the young Lena had time to forge a bond.

*A handbag from the time before designer handbags
became fashionable.*

*The original rocking chair that rocked on a sprung base and not on the floor as in later models. This gave it a much gentler and more rhythmical motion.*

*The Easter 1916 Proclamation which launched the Irish state into a new era.*

*Aunty Peg and Uncle Jacky's wedding in 1932. Aunty Peg told me that prior to going to the church she picked the flowers in her cottage garden and made her own bouquet, and she also decorated the kitchen table for the wedding breakfast.*

A picture of St. Thérèse of Lisieux graced most homes, and this was Aunty Peg's.

S. TERESA DEL BAMBINO GESÙ
CARMELITANA SCALZA
ROMA VIA S. FRANCESCO DI SALES
RIPR. VIETATA          FOT. SCIAMANNA

Many of these jug-and-bowl sets were beautifully decorated and often came with a po to match. They were sometimes accompanied by a white enamel bucket to fetch and carry the water from downstairs up to the bedroom.

Free-range hens were the norm and often frequented the kitchen to peck crumbs off the floor.

The Primus was the first
alternative to the open fire for
boiling the kettle and was fuelled
with oil and lit with the aid of
methylated spirits.

*A lockable decanter holder, which one assumes was to prevent potential tipplers getting access to the spirits.*

Chapter Nine

# Nana Next Door

Aunty Peg never saw herself as a grandmother and, indeed, neither did I, but of course to the people who really mattered – our children – that is exactly who she was. She might not have been their father's birth mother, but to his children living next door that was of no consequence because to them she was a grandmother figure in their world. As she lived so close to us they could escape into her nest when life at home got too bothersome. When Peg's sister-in-law died at a young age and her brother was left with five young children, Peg took the youngest, who would become my husband, under her wing and her husband, Jacky, also welcomed him with open arms. As they had no children of their own, he became their golden boy. Then I came on the scene and his Uncle Jacky decided that I too had a halo, but Aunty Peg had her reservations. And she was right, in many ways, because looking back now I realise that I was any woman's potential nightmare as a daughter-in-law! I was young, opinionated and inexperienced, with a husband who thought that I was perfect and his Uncle Jacky who thought the same.

So it was up to Aunty Peg to put manners on me. And that she did! My mother must have had a premonition that 'coming events cast their shadows before' because she had advised, prior to my moving to Innishannon, 'You are now going to join another family and don't you cause any trouble!' So she was on the look-out for squalls. And when the first baby arrived and I protested that Aunty Peg did not help much with babysitting, I was told, firmly, 'For goodness sake, why should she? He is your child and she knows nothing about small babies.' So I was being taught how to be an appreciative daughter-in-law by a mother who had the experience of having been both daughter-in-law and mother-in-law and was well aware of the potential landmines in that terrain. She also knew that I had a lot to learn. At the time I did not have the maturity to be appreciative, but years later I was grateful for my mother's wisdom because it was the children who benefited in the long run.

*Flaithiúlacht* (generosity) epitomised Peg, as with her there were no half-measures, and her home reflected her generosity. When I was bogged down and laying down the law at home, it was a safe haven for the children. It was a warm, welcoming and comfortable place, and this welcome came too from her two dogs, inappropriately christened Tiny and Topsy. Maybe at an earlier time these names might have been applicable, but those day were long gone. Uncle Jacky, alone, in that entire household was slim, trim and fast-moving. Tiny and Topsy were both enormous, and certainly neither of them was capable of going topsy-turvy. But our children loved them and thought that they were great fun. These dogs were doted on and spoilt rotten, and in between waddles around the little backyard they lay prone on their own individual armchairs. They seldom attempted to climb up the steep path of the long, high, back garden, but stood at the bottom and looked up longingly when Uncle Jacky and Aunty Peg were out gardening or picking fruit, with the children supposedly helping. When Jacky and Peg went out for a walk, Topsy and Tiny, who were too unfit to accompany them, stayed at home in front of the fire, built up specially to keep them warm. Those two dogs had the life of Riley, as had our children when they visited, which they did frequently.

Peg, who was big-hearted and welcoming, had a constant flow of callers, including our children, in and out of her little house behind the shop. There was no front door to her place and the only access was through the shop – and on the way through the children usually benefited from the generosity of Uncle Jacky, who thought that they were angels in disguise.

On Sunday mornings after helping in the shop, they all trooped in and enjoyed big fry-ups of sausages, eggs and rashers bubbling around in a frying pan full of sizzling fat, with burnt toast plastered with layers of melting butter. On other occasions they watched as a red-hot poker was dipped into a jug of porter causing it to sizzle up and generate iron, which Peg deemed very good for them. The warm porter was then doled out into their respective cups, according to their age and size. Peg believed that porter was full of nourishment for children. She loved cooking and the garden provided a constant supply of fresh fruit and vegetables, and the children were bribed with wafer ice cream to help pick gooseberries, raspberries and apples. Later, if they were behaving themselves, they were part of the potting up and sampling of the jam. The henhouse at the top of the garden was another source of great interest as they accompanied her or Uncle Jacky up to feed the hens and collect the eggs.

But it was the making of her apple cakes that generated the most interest. Aunty Peg's apple cake was legendary. It was never confined to a plate, but went into a large, deep roasting pan, big enough to feed all and sundry. The children had competitions as to who could roll the pastry to the right size for the pan. Then they piled the apple slices onto the pastry and had power struggles about who would be allowed to pour in the waterfall of sugar and sprinkle the whole thing with cloves and cinnamon. The covering of the apples varied depending on Peg's mood and the amount of pastry available. It could be made of pastry, or a sponge mixture, or fairy layers. 'Fairy layers' were the best fun because they could be a mixture of everything available.

If the children did not comply with Aunty Peg's regulations they were sent home with a caution of no return, which was soon forgotten. One day, when the youngest was about four, he gave her a cheeky answer. I was summoned to hear her complaint and when I departed the cheeky four-year-old reprimanded her: 'How dare you speak to my mother like that!' Peg thought this was hilarious and called me in that night to report on how he had rushed to my defence. The same young fellow had a vivid imagination and spun tall tales for fun. One evening he burst into her sitting room announcing, 'Maisie has just died!' Now, Maisie was an old neighbour who lived a few doors up the street and he had just passed her on his way into the shop. So he knew full well that she was hail and hearty. He simply wanted to see how Peg would react to his startling news! When she later found out the truth he was banned for days with a threat of a good walloping if he appeared. But he was soon pardoned and later she enjoyed telling Maisie the story of her sudden and unexpected demise.

She and Jacky had a little wobbly house on top of a hill overlooking the bay in Crosshaven and if the children were on their best behaviour they were taken there in Jacky's small mini, or else they got on the bus to Cork and then on a double-decker bus to Crosshaven. This was a huge treat. For each of them, their first trip on the double-decker caused great excitement and was long remembered.

When Jacky died suddenly, Aunty Peg was bereft and as she had never been alone at night the children took turns at sleep-overs. Mainly it was the ten-year-old who moved in to keep her company. The ambience of her bedroom had a monastic theme, ranging from a gigantic Our Lady of Lourdes statue to a multi-coloured Child of Prague, and the pictures on the wall ranged from an angelic St Thérèse of Lisieux pouring down a shower of roses to some tortured-looking saints. At night, Peg's young companion answered the rosary and was introduced to the 'thirty days' prayer'. It was very like my own experience with Nana Ballyduane. Peg, too, was very religious and very republican, so in the following months our ten-year-old was transformed into mixture of Pádraig Pearse and Francis of Assisi. But despite her republican views, she and her best friend went to London from pre-television Ireland to view the pageantry of the royal wedding of then Princess Elizabeth and Prince Philip on television. What a contradiction! But Aunty Peg was into style and grand occasions.

During those months before Aunty Peg died, our ten-year-old and this eighty-year-old must have had some unusual conversations, and in one of them he had obviously got instructions as to which rosary beads were to be put in her hands when she died, and how exactly to arrange them. And when he came home from school on the day she died, he removed the rosary beads that I had in place and did exactly as she had instructed him.

When Aunty Peg died, the boys were sixteen, thirteen,

ten and seven. She had introduced an interesting dimension into their childhood and they each have different memories of her. It was her one regret that we did not have a girl in the family – but within one year of her departure a girl arrived. I think that Aunty Peg had something to do with it.

# Chapter Ten

# Herself Upstairs

She certainly was not the stuff that doting Nanas are made of! During the decade that she lived in our little upstairs apartment, ironically christened the 'West Wing', tales extolling the achievements of her grandchildren never escaped her lips or entered into any of her conversations. And neither was she interested in the activities of other people's grandchildren, even those of her own family, as I discovered one afternoon when one of her long-lost relatives of the same vintage as herself came to visit her. These two cousins had grown up together in the West of Ireland and were meeting up for the first time in many years, so one would have assumed that grandchildren would be a big part of their conversation. But these two ladies had followed very different lifestyles.

The colourful cousin had spent her life in America, and

she arrived in a flurry of flowing garments and large hand-bags. My lady, Mrs C, on the other hand, had lived mostly in France and brought to mind the famous Mrs Simpson – pencil slim, elegant, breathing sophistication, and with a biting wit. Her cousin, having puffed her way upstairs and obtaining a cool, obligatory peck on the cheek, collapsed inelegantly into a fragile, rigid, upright, unreceptive French armchair. I wondered how these two very different ladies were going to pass the afternoon and how their reunion might go.

That evening, when things had quietened in our down-stairs, noisy domain, I called up to see Mrs C. 'Well, Mrs C, how did things go with your cousin?' I enquired. 'Did you have a great afternoon catching up on family matters?' 'Not quite!' she informed me in a cool, measured tone, 'but once we had got one issue sorted, matters did resolve themselves satisfactorily.' 'In what way?' I enquired curiously.

'That woman,' she informed me in an annoyed voice, 'had scarcely collapsed into my chair before she proceeded to open up her enormous handbag and drag out, and proudly display, a photographic procession of bald babies and gowned graduates, in whom I did not have the slightest interest. So when I could no longer tolerate another one, I told her in no uncertain terms to put them all away. There is nothing, I told her, more boring than other people's grandchildren.' This treatment of her long-lost cousin did not surprise me in the least, as it was true to form. She had once informed me: 'In life if you put up with too much you get too much to put up with.' And she certainly adhered to that!

She definitely was not a baby cooer or an admirer of 'bald babies', whether they were of her own family or others. When a young friend who lived next door had a new baby, which, out of sheer courtesy, she brought to visit Mrs C, this young mother later reported with an amused, understanding smile: 'We have been inspected! No cooing and billing over newborns from Mrs C!'

Born into one of the great houses in the West of Ireland, and, having spent most of her life living in England and France, she spent her last decade in our house, to which she brought a flavour of 'arsenic and old lace'. Upstairs, in a little apartment, which one of our sons had absurdly christened 'The West Wing', though it was a million miles from such spacious grandeur, she proceeded to try to put manners on my unruly crew, from whom she tolerated no nonsense.

She arrived into their lives in her late seventies when two of our children were pre-teens and another two early teens, which was a pretty challenging age combination. Though she would have shuddered at the very idea of it, during the years she spent with us she evolved into a kind of 'upstairs grandmother-in-residence' figure. Though holding totally opposing political views, she and my own grandmother were women cut from the same weave, and their rigidity and intractability illustrated how complicated and difficult relationships can become.

She insisted that the children did exactly as she instructed while in her domain. She enjoyed the company of youth and loved good conversation, and to that end strove to keep them up to speed on current world events. She read *The Times* and *Daily Mail* every day, pronouncing that she abhorred the decline of journalism especially during the 'silly season'. But while she enjoyed having young ones around her, patience was not one of her virtues and clipped retorts, akin to those of the Dowager Duchess in Downton Abbey, often whipped them into shape and put them in their place. 'Racing Demon' was a two-player game of patience that she taught them in an allotted time with her, which they slotted in between school lessons and shop duties. Now, whatever the agreed time, punctuality was key with Mrs C. When she specified a time, she meant that time – on the dot! One night she decided to begin teaching them how to play Bridge, and they were invited up to her West Wing at 8pm, but when they appeared five minutes before the appointed time they were promptly dismissed with the instruction to return at the correct time. A few nights later, one of them made the mistake of referring to the fact that he had learnt to play Bridge to be sharply reprimanded: 'Young man, you have never learned to play Bridge. You are always learning.' She insisted on good behaviour on all occasions, and insisted too that on social occasions you needed 'to bring you penny to the pool' and take part as best you could, offering something interesting to the gathering. A great lesson for children! She herself admitted to three vices: whiskey on the rocks, pure dark chocolate and Silk Cut cigarettes, from which she strongly advised them to abstain.

Sometimes while she was away on holiday, the one who got on best with her would drag a bucket of white emulsion up to the West Wing to eradicate the traces of yellow nicotine stains from her walls.

She went on long holidays all over the world. Her final one was to Russia, where she planned to visit selected art galleries. When one of her friends demurred as to the wisdom of such a daunting undertaking at her age and of the possibly of her demise so far from home, these protestations were acidly dismissed with the dry comment, 'I'm sure that people die in Russia too.'

When her final departure did come, she achieved it with as little fuss as possible, thus ending a decade of training in good behaviour, card-playing, camaraderie and companionship for her 'downstairs grandchildren'.

Chapter Eleven

# Half-way House

S he was nobody's Nana but most people around the village called her Nana. She lived on Bóthar na Sop, which translated means 'road of the sop' (a 'sop' being a hand-ful of hay or straw). Its name came from pre-famine times when both sides of that boreen were edged with thatched cottages. Now it is a sheltered, looped, leafy lane at the east-ern end of Innishannon village, and a little further on it links back to the main road outside the village. In Nana's time – the 1950s and 1960s – there were only two houses there, including hers, whereas now there are over thirty family homes there, with large gardens attached. Nana and her little house are long gone, but in the evenings as I walk along there I remember her because of my young friends Sean and Timmy, to whom she was a real Nana figure.

When I came to the village in the early sixties it took me

a few years before I got into the rhythm of village living. And strangely enough, it was these two little boys, who lived at the other end of the village, who helped me find my feet. In the unexplainable way that village life works, we drifted across each other and somehow or other adopted each other. Their mother had died at a young age and I was a bit rudderless, being new to the village, so maybe we had a common need. Sean was then eight years of age and Timmy was six. They were bright, happy, chatty little lads and took to calling daily to my house. They were full of fun, and in due course when my firstborn arrived, they became my baby minders.

Every afternoon they came and the new arrival, like any first baby, was dressed up in an immaculate new outfit. They took him out for a drive in his pristine new buggy. They arrived back a few hours later with the pristine baby having undergone an amazing transformation: his once-spotless blue and white outfit and the buggy were different shades of brown and grey, and covered in varying degrees of black soot. They had been visiting Nana – and all had had a great time!

Sean and Timmy and their father were regular callers to Nana's house. They would walk up Bóthar na Sop and drop in to say hello. Her door was always open and the cast-iron kettle was always hanging on the crook in the big old fireplace where you could actually sit by the side of the fire, under the chimney, and look up at the sky.

Nana sat in her chair, which was a seat made out of an

old car seat, which at the time was not unusual, and urged one of them to scald the 'taypot and wet the tay'. Nana didn't speak English or Irish, but a combination of both, which confused people who did actually speak Irish. She also frequently used a combination of English and Irish swear words. On one occasion, when she visited Sean and Timmy's home in the village, little Timmy repeated a swear word that he had heard her use, but she proceeded to question everyone in the room as to where her small 'gorsoon' could have heard such a bad word!

She was a constant smoker of Woodbines cigarettes, which were unfiltered and untipped, and she would smoke these down to the very end – so much so that she would have to blow the end out as there would not be enough left to take from between her fingers. Nana never used a match to light her cigarette but would bend down and pick up a hot piece of coal or timber from the fire in her fingers and light her cigarette that way. She would then discard the hot ember back into the fireplace with a litany of colourful Gaelic swear words. Nana's capacity for enduring heat was amazing and she could spear a boiling potato from the black iron pot which hung on the crook over the fire and would put the potato on the glowing embers for a few minutes – and would then pick it up with her bare hands and proceed to eat it with relish. No need for a knife and fork when you had fingertips like hers.

Nana was a small, squat lady, with very dark hair and skin. She seemed to shuffle along rather than walk, but this was probably due to her wearing large boots, which were kinder to her feet than smaller, tight-fitting shoes. She wore a wrap-around apron over a long black dress, which was very much the fashion for older women of that time. She originally came from the Old Head of Kinsale and she loved to tell her 'grandchildren' stories of her young life by the sea.

One of the most memorable stories she told them was of the sinking of the *Lusitania* in 1915 which resulted in the loss of nearly 1200 lives. The *Lusitania*, an English passenger ship, was torpedoed off the Old Head of Kinsale while on its way to Liverpool from New York City. The eight hundred survivors were brought ashore and taken to Cobh, then known as Queenstown. The catastrophe left long-lasting memories on the minds of the people living along that seashore. Nana told of the various things that were washed ashore by the incoming tide around the Old Head. Some of the local men ventured out to sea in their small boats and salvaged items that were afloat. She recalled the shoals of compressed meats and other foodstuffs that were found. Some of these foods were strange to the local taste, but the locals lived off the supply for months.

In the spring Nana would summon the children to gather the spring nettles. According to her, boiled nettles were the cure for all ailments. She would show the children how to differentiate between the fresh spring nettles and the old ones. She assured them that the spring nettles would never sting, but contrary to her opinion while picking a canister of nettles they would get well and truly stung! The next time she would ask them to pick, they might show a little reluctance, but she would convince them that they had not got any stings the previous week – and so they picked and ate nettles as the spring rolled on.

Her house was very welcoming for anyone passing to or from Innishannon. During the day, many of the older ladies, having gone to the village for their messages, were glad to call in for tea and a chat on their way home, which afforded them a good rest before embarking on the further two or three miles with their weekly shopping. Evening time was male time, and the husbands of the ladies who called during the day, or the bachelor farmers who were on the way to one of the four pubs in the village, dropped in to discuss local and international news. A number of times every year a travelling man would come and stay in one of the sheds adjacent to Nana's house while he canvassed the locality for pots, pans and buckets to mend. He was known as 'The Tinker' and his was a very essential service at that time.

In later years when she became ill, Nana was taken to St Finbarr's Hospital in Cork where Sean went to visit her. But on arrival he went from bed to bed looking for her, and having visited each bed figured out that he must be in the wrong ward or else Nana had been moved. He inquired from a nurse and she assured him that Nana was in that particular ward and she directed him to a bed which he had checked minutes earlier. In the bed was an unrecognisable Nana, resting peacefully in a guise he had never seen before: a pristine lady with shining silver hair and beautiful, angelic white skin. But when she opened her eyes and greeted him with a flow of Gaelic, he knew then that this was his Nana from Innishannon.

Nana died a few days later, leaving many happy memories with Sean and Timmy and the many visitors who, over the years, had visited her half-way house – and called her Nana.

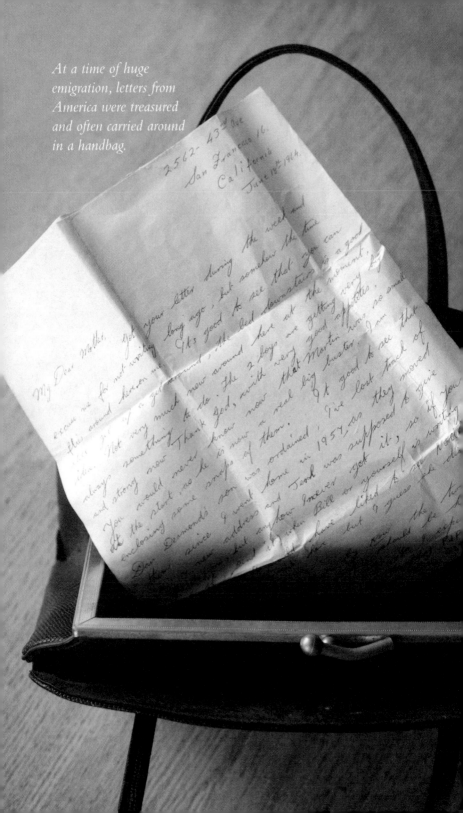

At a time of huge
emigration, letters from
America were treasured
and often carried around
in a handbag.

*These thick, heavy, glass bottles are embossed with: J. Walsh & Company Bandon, and E. Cades and Sons Cork.*

*This hung in our shop here in Innishannon and is an example of our beautiful old Gaelic lettering.*

*A statue of Our Lady graced most homes and was always part of the May altar.*

This old mantel clock peals out melodious chimes every quarter hour.

*Aunty Peg's old prayerbook. Most old prayerbooks were chock-a-block with favourite prayers and old mortuary cards.*

*An enamel soap dish which was once part of a bedroom set belonging to my mother.*

*Pipe smoking was a common practice and advertisements extolling its virtues were commonplace, as in this one from our shop.*

Chapter Twelve

# Nana Theresa

And now it was our turn. Our Nanas had endeavoured to hand on their deep faith, a respect for the natural world and the importance of the extended family. Their strong belief in a divine creator had sustained them through tough times, their respect for the natural world had preserved the environment and by keeping in touch with family members at home and abroad they strove to preserve the family heritage. That was their legacy – and what, one wonders, will be ours?

When my sister Theresa became a young grandmother, she changed the face of that role in our family. She was a far cry from the Peig Sayers Nana-by-the-fire sort of grandmother. She was Super-Nana to the children of one of her daughters, and her mode of operation resembled Nana Ballyduane rather more than our own mother. She was full of energy and determination, and all her grandchildren soon learned that it was 'her way or the high way'.

She drove them around in her green Starlet car, the boot choked with golf clubs, bags of potting compost and baby buggies. Her overture on arrival was a scattering of gravel and the smell of burning rubber. She would come to take them to school, her wheels spinning on take-off in her hurry, and collect them in the evening smelling of scorched clutch. She was always on the go at a fast pace. On their return from school she filled them with hot dinners and bowls of steaming, creamy, thick custard laced with copious amounts of sugar. They loved the custard, but this was held back until all dinner plates were licked clean. When they were at home from school, sick, she nurtured them with comforting food. One of their favourites was rice pudding, which she made in a saucepan with milk, and she sometimes mixed blackberry jam in with the warm rice. A great favourite was pandy, which was hot mashed potatoes mixed with lumps of butter, salt and onion, and she turned it into colcannon by adding cabbage to the mix – even though she was the ultra-modern grandmother there was a throwback to former habits. In the summer they got dishes of jelly as she always had big sections of jelly and blocks of ice cream in her fridge.

With both their parents working, their Nana was often

in charge. She was a powerhouse, with endless energy and a positive attitude, and she could decide to do anything at a moment's notice. Some days they came home from school to a totally transformed house because their Nana would be in a 'clear the clutter' mode and they would be greeted with the smell of furniture polish, a glowing fire, shining worktops, mopped floors and windows gleaming after an encounter with Mr Muscle. They believed that nobody could clear clutter like their Nana! She put a *snas* (polish) on everything and could make an ordinary day feel extraordinary.

It would not be an unusual occurrence for their parents to come back to a house that was totally rearranged. They might leave the house in the morning closing a sober, brown door behind them, and come home in the evening to a brilliant yellow welcome! A tired carpet might have disappeared from a bedroom and the concrete floor painted, garden furniture transformed and brought into use as homework tables. And if a pair of curtains was looking sad, she might drive to the local draper's shop, purchase a roll of fabric and come home to her sewing machine – and by evening have a new pair of curtains hanging. She was a whizz with her Singer sewing machine and the children felt that she could transform even an old hessian potato sack into a party dress – and she could! She just 'had it' when it came to sewing and she made it all look effortless. If a warm summer's day dawned ahead of schedule, their long pants could be cut into shorts in a flash and expertly hemmed up with her sewing

machine. In some of her undertakings they were her reluctant accomplices, knowing that their parents might not be
too impressed with Nana's redecorating of their house. But
by then, Nana would be gone out the gate with a screech of
brakes and a swirl of gravel. She didn't entertain any objec-
tions and with her it was always full steam ahead.

Once when they were attending a local summer camp
for five- to seven-year-olds a fancy dress parade was the
big event for the final day. No problem for their Nana! She
arrived the day before with many different types of fab-
rics including leopard-print faux fur, chiffon, rolls of mesh
and beautiful silky red ribbons. The whole evening was a
whirl of activity, with Nana busily making outfits for all of
them and their friends. Within a few hours a Fred Flintstone and Miss Marigold and others were born. One had a
lovely bonnet with red ribbon, a top and skirt of mesh that
bounced when she twirled and Fred Flintstone came forth
in a furry hat and a kind of toga. Nana had created magic, as
usual. The following day they were delighted to come home
with many prizes, much to Nana's satisfaction.

The two words these children most loved to hear from
Nana were 'Mystery Tour'. These mystery tours could take
them anywhere and their imaginations used to go wild in
anticipation about the possibilities of where they might
finish up. They loved Millstreet Country Park, and sometimes they went further afield to Killarney. One mystery
tour took them to a second-hand shop and they were fascinated as to what they might find in there. Nana parked

outside and they all jumped out of the car. Full of curiosity they shot in the door of the shop leaving Nana to follow. Suddenly they heard a loud bang and crashing glass, and they ran back out in alarm. Glass was flying up into the air and an irate man was shouting. Nana's car door had been blown off by a passing truck. They thought that Nana was dead! They started screaming at the man: 'Is Nana dead? Is Nana dead?' But, like James Bond walking away from a disaster scene, their unfazed Nana emerged from the car into a sea of glass on the road around her and quickly calmed their hysterical crying. Luckily, next to the second-hand shop was a sweet shop, and the kind owner, who was a golfing friend of Nana's, calmed and soothed them with a tsunami of sweets. Nana's car got a makeover in the form of a new door, slightly darker than the original colour, but this only added to the character and uniqueness of Nana's green bus.

Gardening was one of the great loves of her life and she regularly dragged the children out to help, telling them that the secret of good gardening was 'to keep the shovel tipping'. As a gardener, she was a blend of nurturer and excavator. With their reluctant assistance, a complete rose bed could be moved from one end of the garden to the other in one day. To encourage their cooperation, Nana was a great believer in bribery and blackmail – and it always worked! No job was too daunting and once begun it somehow always got finished, if not by Nana, then by someone else who could not bear looking at the mess.

Her grandchildren were very proud of their Nana who

always looked great and was very glamorous. Even now she is still a huge presence in their lives, a force to be reckoned with, and she always has a positive mental attitude, regardless of the situation. Like her own grandmother, Nana Ballyduane, my sister Theresa is a woman of action and maybe the same criteria can be applied to her as were applicable to Nana Ballyduane: 'She would kill you and she would cure you.' So maybe the family gene lives on and the belief that she has tried to instill in her grandchildren is: 'You can if you think you can'. Maybe not such a bad legacy for life.

# Chapter Thirteen

# Lathered with Love

Theresa and Thomas, my sister Theresa's other grand-children, were blessed for many years with having two grandmothers as part of their lives. That these were two very different kinds of grandmother brought variety to the grandmother role. Their maternal grandmother, Nana Theresa, kept them on their toes and was constantly issuing new challenges, whereas their paternal grandmother, Granny Collins, was unquestioning in her adoration of them and they knew they could do no wrong in her eyes!

Theresa's earliest memory of her Granny Collins was of having her hair brushed by her and she knew that her Granny loved to do this and always told Theresa that her hair was beautiful that it should always be long. One time the local hairdresser took off more than the routine '1 inch' and this led to young Theresa going into hiding behind the sofa, refusing to be seen in public, and wearing a hat to school for a week! Granny made her promise never to let anyone cut her lovely hair that short again. The six-year-old Theresa took this promise very seriously and to this day her hair has never been above shoulder length!

Their Granny and her son, their Uncle Thomas, would come to visit every second Sunday night and there was high excitement preceding their arrival. While Theresa was telling me this her face lit up with a smile of remembrance at the buzz in the house before their visitors came. As children their concept of time was still in its early days, so they knew the time by which TV show was on and would take it in turns to check outside for any sign of headlights. Then when the 6pm News was on they knew that the doorbell would go at any minute.

On Granny's arrival Theresa remembers that they were like two puppies crowding around her wanting to get their hugs in straight away. Then they would all sit down around the table and have a special tea, and toast was always part of this meal as Granny loved toast. Bread went under the grill and they all made sure that it did not burn. The smell of toast filled the kitchen, with slices piled high in the middle of the table. Even when a toaster came into the house they still used the grill, as a toaster could only do two slices at a time and that wasn't enough! Sometimes both grill and toaster were kept busy during Granny's visits.

When the tea was over it was on to the washing up. This was a ritual where Granny sat on a chair by the sink and would carefully dry the ware that they had washed, all the while chatting about her neighbours. Theresa always enjoyed hearing these stories and finding out what was going on in Granny's world.

Granny always brought 'goodies' for them. Out of her bag came fizzy orange and an old butter tub filled to the brim with little treat-sized bars. For the entire week Theresa and Thomas would ration that fizzy orange, enjoying each bit of sugar rushing through their veins. Theresa felt that their health-conscious parents did not approve, but they never said a word.

Visiting Granny at her home was always fun. In pride of place above the fireplace was a framed photo of Theresa and Thomas. This made them feel they were very loved and very special.

The mysterious back kitchen always captured their imaginations. It was one of those wonderful but peculiar rooms where you felt like you were outside though you were actually inside. There were biscuit tins on high shelves with hidden treasures and these tins often produced many wonderful surprises. One of these was a wind-up dog which had been one of their Dad's favourite toys. Theresa and Thomas would sit up on a wooden bench at the kitchen table and squeal with delight as the dog's legs moved rapidly, taking it from one end of the table to the other! While they played, they would be given the royal treatment of a glorious spread of custard creams, bourbon biscuits and fizzy orange.

Granny loved telling stories about their Dad, and they

loved hearing them. It helped them to bridge the generations and enter into their father's young world. Children love hearing about a parent's childhood. It's a wonderful gift from a grandparent to a child.

Granny loved to 'stand to' them. She would furtively slip some money into the palms of their hands as if she were partaking in some illegal activity. They never refused, of course, and were delighted to get it. Theresa now understands that Granny was discreetly giving them this money on the quiet so that their parents wouldn't make them give it back! They loved the financial freedom her money gave them and would plot and plan what to do with their money. In the year 2000 they hatched a plan to save up all their 'Granny money' to buy a Playstation 2. When they reached the target they couldn't believe it – it just showed how generous Granny was to them! When Granny called to visit on the Sunday after the big purchase, Theresa remembers taking her by the hand to show her what she had bought them! Granny was kind and interested, and sat down to watch them play some games. When Theresa looks back now it makes her smile to think of the generation difference and how their eighty-five-year-old Granny really had no idea what a Playstation was but made them feel like she knew exactly what was going on.

When she was saying goodbye at the end of each visit she would try to prepare them for the fact that the day would come when she would no longer come visiting them, but they never thought that the day would actually come. But on 15 November 2001 Granny Collins passed away in her sleep. Theresa had never experienced grief before and was shocked by the realisation that she would never again talk to her beloved Granny. That evening they drove down to her home in Newcestown and there was Granny in her bed, holding her hot water bottle and still warm. This is a memory for which Theresa is very grateful. Her Granny looked cosy and peaceful. Seeing her like this made her death seem not so scary. It was her time to go. She had loved them so much and even now, twenty years later, Theresa still feels that love.

Theresa believes that though a person physically dies the relationship you had with them does not. Her first experience of death was of Granny Collins and it taught her this. For every exam and interview Theresa has done she has brought a necklace belonging to her Granny along with her. She often has a quick chat and asks for support and always feels that Granny pulls her through.

She remembers that in her handbag Granny always carried her little crucifix. She would often take it out, place it in Theresa's hand and they would say a special prayer together. Even after all these years Theresa still remembers her Granny's prayer.

> A little metal crucifix
> As plain as it could be
> But only God in heaven knows
> How dear it is to me …

In later years Theresa realised how much she cherished those intimate moments. She feels they were so lucky to have such a wonderful Granny in their lives and she hopes Granny would be proud of the adults that she helped them become.

# Chapter Fourteen

# Hi Ref!

When I think of dedicated Nanas, my sister-in-law, Agnes, immediately comes to mind. She was an absolutely dedicated Nana! And it evidenced itself in many ways.

When photographs for our annual Christmas village magazine *Candlelight* begin to come in, there could be amongst them some old photos of local football or hurling teams with unknown faces lined up amongst the players around the winning trophy. Then it is necessary to make contact with people around the parish who might be able to identify these forgotten faces. Those who can do this are usually the 'die hard' GAA parish veterans, with long memories of each match, who can recall every puck of the ball. These dedicated men – usually men – wedded to the sporting cause are in every GAA club in the country. I was married to one, and his sister, Agnes, was right up there too amongst these dedicated stalwarts who knew everyone who had played with our local club, The Valley Rovers. Agnes always came good. It was a case of 'Where the heart lies there the treasure is.' She knew everything that was of interest to her sporting grandchildren.

Her sporting involvement began at an early age when, as a brilliant young camogie player, she was head-hunted by the local lads' team to don a disguising head gear and play with them in a vital final! She took on the challenge, but her outstanding hurling skills and unique technique soon drew the attention of the opposing team, who alerted the referee, which led to eventual recognition. She was unceremoniously dispatched to the sideline by a referee perplexed by the rarity of whatever rule she was deemed to have broken.

When her own playing days were over she was replaced by an equally skilful daughter and six sons, with whom she played from the sideline. The majority of these offspring married within the parish, so she finished up with enough grandchildren to field her own team. For each one of them, she was a dedicated sideline supporter and was not shy on alerting an offending referee of his lack of alertness on observing and chastising a misdemeanour committed by the opposing team. With years of match experience under her belt, she was an expert on hard-earned frees and the entitlement of a player to a sideline cut. Before a referee had time to blow his whistle and point out which way the ball was going he was informed from the sideline 'That's a Rovers' ball.' And because she knew every rule of the game down to the finest detail, she was invariably right, and not reticent in hammering home her point.

Her interest was not confined to the GAA but spread across the sporting board to soccer and rugby and if any of her grandchildren happened to be playing any of those games distance was no obstacle to her attendance. But the GAA was probably her first love and she travelled all over the country to games and was a regular attendee at All-Ireland finals. Competitive by nature, she loved the thrill of a good game – but if Cork was playing she only saw red.

She was an absolutely dedicated grandmother. Her deep-rooted love of children probably stretched back to her own childhood. Her mother died when Agnes was a little girl, so she had grown up acutely aware of the huge importance of a mother and a grandmother in the life of a child. And she was not found wanting, but dedicated years to babysitting and driving grandchildren to school and to matches. She was part of all their upbringings and her home was the nucleus of the extended family. Every Sunday evening all the grand-children and their parents gathered there. Her large living room was filled with noisy games and chatter, and even-tually the adults would retire to the kitchen where they could converse in peace while the younger ones dragged out boxes of old games and odds and ends that Agnes had collected over the years, and which they had converted into toys. During the evening she invariably gravitated back into the room full of noisy grandchildren where she became part of the games, always joining forces with the one she saw as not doing as well as the others. Sometimes she just sat and chatted with them. In the summer their activities took them out into the field beside the house to play ball games, and Agnes would play pitcher in their games of rounders or would spike the ball for them in volleyball. If one of them was doing especially well she was quite capable of sneaking up and tripping them to give the smaller ones a chance to pull even!

They referred to the older half of the cousins as 'The Biggies' and the younger ones as 'The Smallies'. Because of all these weekly gatherings, The Biggies and The Smallies now feel that they all grew up as siblings rather than cousins because Nana Agnes was so involved in taking care of them all and played a huge part in their upbringing. She made them feel like one big family.

So the little girl who grew up without a mother or grandmother had made it her goal in life to became a dedicated mother and grandmother – and she certainly played a blinder.

*Lace-making and crochet were common practices and samples of their Nana's skills are now prized by many grandchildren.*

*Sewing boxes, sometimes homemade as in this case, were part of every home.*

*Before central heating, patchwork quilts were part of bedroom requirements and now tell the story of times past.*

There was a Singer sewing machine in most homes and if you did not have one of your own you brought your sewing to a neighbour who had.

These figurines between her
candlesticks were part of Aunty
Peg's bit and pieces.

*Knitting and darning were part of the nightly activities around the open fire.*

*My mother's handbag, which was her hold-all for all her necessities when going to town.*

*Over the fireplace hangs a picture of Grandmother Taylor, flanked by Nana Taylor and her granddaughter Lena.*

Chapter Fifteen

# Till the Cows Come Home

Nowadays when I awaken in the morning I can tell the time by the sound of the passing traffic. The slight humming sound is not intrusive, just the background murmur to our village life today. Some years back, this sound commenced around 8.30am, but has gradually got earlier and now begins at 6am. People's days have lengthened and the flow of passing traffic has increased and accelerated. But it was not always like this.

When I came to live in the village in the early 1960s it was cows, not cars, that announced the beginning of a new day. At that time, some of the village people owned fields outside the village, but the stalls for milking and winter housing of these cows lay behind their village homes where there were large gardens and yards. In summer, the cows were brought into the village, morning and evening, to be milked and it was customary to see an entire herd of cows ambling leisurely along the street to eventually meander in an open gate for milking. These cows were not to be hurried and instinctively knew that this was their place and stoically ignored any rare vehicle that attempted to speed up or hinder their slow amble to their milking place.

Across the road from my house was one such yard attached to a pub, and those now-abandoned cow stalls currently provide storage for outdoor dining tables and chairs. A gracious old house further up the street, with a huge garden running down to the river, had a second spacious yard further along the street to which their cows returned daily to be milked by the woman of the house. That cow house has now been transformed into the village café, so this yard has gone from housing cows to catering for humans. Another little street house had the use of a large field at the western end of the village where the man of the house had what in today's world would be termed a market garden, and it also had sufficient grazing and hay for cows that provided milk for a large percentage of the village. This field was and still is known as The Bleach because an English landlord in earlier times bleached linen there, and it is now our GAA pitch and home to the local playground. On my kitchen dresser stands a jug once owned by my husband's Aunty Peg, and he remembered being sent across the road as a child to this house, bearing the jug to be filled with milk, with a strict warning not to drop it. Now, as I carefully take this jug down off the dresser shelf, I remember Aunty Peg's caution and I too am careful. It is an elegant jug and ideal for holding bunches of garden flowers. A further milk supply was provided by the daughters of a farm on the edge of the village who milked the cows and delivered gallons of milk daily around the village before going to school.

In the middle of the village was the Mill, to which the farmers bought their grain for milling, and that area is now a car sales depot. At the eastern end a historic old Market House still graces the village to which, at an earlier time, the farmers brought their produce to market. To this Market House in earlier times, John Wesley came to preach, and later it was sometimes used as a makeshift cinema or theatre for travelling play groups, and the audience came carrying their own chairs and cushions. As well as this beautiful old building, two elegant steeples towering above the trees add stature to the village skyline. In these two churches down through the years the village people divided to pray to the same God. But in recent times when St Mary's Catholic church was being renovated the Catholic congregation went up the street into the Church of Ireland building to celebrate Mass, and when Christ Church was being reno-vated its congregation was welcomed to hold their service in St Mary's Catholic Church. Thankfully, we have moved on from our rigid, intolerant religious thinking, and now a retired Church of Ireland clergyman comes daily to the Catholic church to say his prayers. A big step forward from the times when we did not even consider stepping inside the door of each other's churches.

Just beyond the Market House was a poultry business to which people brought their eggs for sale and also came to acquire and sell chickens and hens. All the village homes had large gardens that they cultivated, and many kept hens too, and those with access to the river kept ducks and some kept pigs. This was the world in which the village Nanas played a large part as it was the Nanas, helped by the children, who looked after the hens, ducks, pigs and also milked the cows. Some Nanas had empty nests as their children had emigrated and during the summer their grandchildren, often with English accents, came to spend their holidays with their Irish Nana, and played and made friends with the village children and with other children also holidaying with their Nanas. Friendships were forged that lasted a lifetime.

Chapter Sixteen

# Riverside House

There was only one house in Innishannon for which I would consider leaving my own house. It was right across the road from me but nearer to the western end of the village. It was a large, roomy, warm grandmother of a house which, on first sighting, would bring a smile to your face. Even though it was located on the side of the street, this house had stepped back a little as if to give itself breathing space from the comings and goings out front. This set it apart from the other street houses – and as if that was not enough, it had over its Georgian front door a glass-enclosed balcony from where you could sit and watch the world go by. On either side of this balcony were two twinkling windows matching the two beneath on either side of a beautiful recessed doorway. It was set apart from the house on its right by a high garden wall, and a wide slipway to the river on its left separated it from the house at the other side. Fittingly christened Riverside House, its large south-facing garden ran right down to the river. It had doors on either side of its spacious hall leading into two large rooms looking out over the street. Back the corridor brought you to a large room on the left and then the jewel in the crown to the right: a wonderful kitchen looking down over the garden that ran right to the river bank. From the kitchen you could look across the water at Dromkeen Wood. It was a dream house, old, mellowed, and at peace with itself and its surroundings. And in this house lived one of the village Nanas. Her house was a place in which to create wonderful memories, and this it did for her Dublin grandchildren, who, every summer during their growing years, came and spent their holidays here with their grandmother. They called her 'Grawn'.

Their grandmother had been born on a farm just outside the village – her grandchildren were not quite sure of the exact date as she never divulged it, but they thought that it could have been 1894 or 1896. She had met their Grandpa, whom they called 'Boss', in 1920 when he was home on leave from his job as a policeman on colonial service in Natal, South Africa. Being a policeman on foreign service meant extended leave every three years of around three to four months. During one of these leaves their grandmother had gone out to East London and they got married. They returned to Ireland in 1933 when their grandfather's thirty-year service gave him a full pension. Initially they lived in Kinsale, but eventually bought Riverside House on the main street in Innishannon. With the house came a large yard further down the street where they kept cows. In later years their daughter, Mavourneen, went to work in Dublin where she got married and had six children, who came to Innishannon every summer and spent their entire holidays with their grandmother in Riverside House.

These children loved the holidays in Riverside House. Their Gran was warm, gregarious and chatty and many visitors came and went as their Gran had many beloved friends, neighbours and relatives, all of whom they got to know over the years. Their day would start with breakfast – but not before their dawn chorus of 'Good morning, Grawn darling.' Then they'd have a breakfast of hen's eggs – 'guggies'– porridge and soda bread. A ritual in the house was roasted coffee beans, a habit from South Africa, and then tea for the rest of the day. Coffee was only for the morning.

Also having breakfast with them was their Great Uncle Peter, a large man with a hearty guffaw of a laugh, who had retired to Innishannon after a long career in the Post and Telegraphs' Department as the principal buyer of telegraph poles for the state and the Irish telephone distribution system. In the 1930s and 40s he travelled widely, especially to Finland, on his log-purchasing duties. For the children he was a fount of knowledge on many things, including the names of the many trees that lined the opposite riverbank at the bottom of their Gran's garden. Their Gran kept hens and ducks, and the ducks would go on the river every day – and return up the slip that divided Riverside House from the house next door. The ducks waited outside the shed door every night to be let in for feeding and safety from the fox. Their Uncle Peter always enjoyed duck eggs for breakfast.

Their neighbours on the right had a houseful of young children and over the years they all became best friends and they played every day in the Bleach (now the GAA pitch) and swam in the river. The man of the house next door kept bees and those bees loved their Gran's garden of beautiful flowers. In summer the bees were everywhere but none of the children ever got stung.

The routine of Riverside House began at dawn. The cows had to be brought down from a field outside the village by their Aunty Trish, down a boreen called Bóthar na Sop into the cow shed, milked by their Gran, and then returned back up Bóthar an Sop to the field. The milk was put into a churn and collected regularly by the creamery.

Throughout the day people came and went to Riverside House. A daily visitor was Michael John, a cattle jobber who lived in the village, and who came in to read the *Irish Independent* at the kitchen table. His glamorous niece Patsy often dropped in after coming home by bus from Cork where she worked in hospitality. She was exquisitely coiffured, beautiful and delightful, and the children were captivated by her glamour and personality. All the neighbours were regular callers, including a visiting family who came home from England every summer to holiday in Innishannon with their grandaunts who lived across the road.

Many of their Gran's relations, who were farmers, often

came by – with spuds and vegetables, and, most important of all, the local news. Gran's niece, Julia, was a particular favourite and she filled them in on all that was going on around the parish. Gran's sister, Aunty Moll, was another visitor whom they were always delighted to see. A most important caller every Friday was Mr White, the fishmonger, who brought mackerel. The children loved to watch their Gran fillet the fish and prepare it for their dinner. The cats outside would paw at the large kitchen window, knowing the treat they would get later – the heads and entrails for a sumptuous feast. The children thought that their Gran was a magician with mackerel. They loved it. SuperGran wasn't in it with their Gran.

Another relative who always visited on his holidays was their Gran's nephew from Cape Town, South Africa. He was a late vocation to the priesthood after the war, having served in the South African army and been captured in Tobruk, Libya, in 1942 – he became a prisoner of war until 1945. Later he studied in the Beda College in Rome, and came to Cork every summer until his ordination in 1951. He was a genial, happy man, who loved Maw, as he called their Gran.

In the late fifties when they came on holiday there was another resident in the house. A new doctor had come to stay because he knew a cousin of their Gran's. The Doc, as he became known, introduced the phone to Gran – they had a phone downstairs and a plug-in one upstairs, in what became known as the Doc's Room. This was very advanced for the time. The Doc had an Irish setter called Ronnie and the children loved him. They were thrilled at his amazing speeds down the Bleach – wow! The Doc was great fun. He would come in late, dressed up as a tramp, and do pretend stuff to confuse them. They knew it was him – but couldn't prove it, though Gran always gave it away by her laughter. The Doc was very mischievous, and very loved by all in Innishannon for his kindness and medical skills.

During their annual holidays in Innishannon these Dublin children got to know everybody in the village and as they grew older some of them worked with us here in our guest house. They were full of fun and great workers. In later years, when their beloved Gran had passed away and the old house was sold, they still came back to visit Innishannon and meet the many friends they had made during those long summer holidays.

The memory of their much-loved Gran and their long, idyllic summer holidays in Innishannon enriched their lives and stayed with them forever.

Chapter Seventeen

# They Called Her Nan

The presence of a grandmother in the life of a child who has lost their mother is probably of huge significance. I knew that the sudden death of my friend Phil's mother when Phil was a child caused her a lot of pain. She was nine and her brother, Paddy, seven, and their mother in her mid-forties. This was a devastating blow and had a profound affect on all of them. She still remembers clearly Paddy and herself being taken into a room in the hospital where she kept asking for her father. After what seemed an interminably long time, her father came into the room and Phil sensed immediately that something terrible had happened: he was crying, and it was the first time Phil had ever seen an adult crying. In that room her world collapsed and her childhood evaporated. But despite this early trauma – or maybe because of it – Phil grew up to become a woman of

176

amazing resourcefulness and compassion.

In every community there are people who are reliable and dependable, who help to steady the boat in stormy waters and to keep the show on the road despite prevailing squalls. This is Phil! A woman of substance blessed with an innate ability 'not to lose the head' in an emergency and cope calmly amidst chaos and confusion. Add to this, years of nursing and later working in a centre for adults traumatised by alcohol and drugs, and you have someone skilled in coming to the rescue when trouble strikes. This is why Phil is a person whom I, like many of our friends, can ring in stressful situations.

I first got to know Phil many years ago when she was roped in to judge a baby show – which in today's world would be deemed totally politically incorrect but at the time was an accepted fund-raiser in a carnival run by the local GAA club. She got landed with this job because at the time she lived outside the parish, which meant that she would be safe if she ruffled any feathers. But Phil handled the entire undertaking with such diplomacy and kindness that she had all the babies and us mammies feeling like winners.

Some years later Phil married a local farmer and came to live in Innishannon and was soon immersed in many parish organisations, including Community Alert and many Church activities. When our parish was reduced to one very overworked priest, who could not be available on all occasions, it was Phil who received a funeral cortege at the church door with compassion and sensitivity, and afterwards led the rosary and comforted the mourners. What a wonderful opportunity our Church missed out on when in deciding to ordain deacons they did not include women like Phil. It was the perfect time to move forward inclusively. In Innishannon, as in every parish, there are some great women who would have enriched the Church in so many ways.

I was aware that there had been a Nana in Phil's background. One day, when she and I talked about her childhood, I was introduced to her memories of her grandmother. This grandmother, whom Phil called Nan, was in her early seventies when Phil entered her life. She was Phil's paternal grandmother and she lived with them in their home where Phil's father worked the family farm. Phil was her first grandchild and her Nan was also her godmother. She was called after her grandmother, as was the custom of the times. Her Nan was present at Phil's christening the day after she was born in the Erinville hospital in Cork. The christening was held in a city church and baby Phil was returned to the hospital after the christening, as was the usual practice then.

Phil's earliest memory of Nan was sitting on her lap and Nan stroking her head. Phil had wavy hair and Nan liked to put it into ringlets. Nan herself had long hair, which was always tied in a plait around the back of her head. The plait was kept in place with hairpins, which fascinated Phil and her little brother Paddy, and Nan also wore a dark brown hairnet covering her head. Her hair was auburn in colour and Phil remembers that she scarcely had any grey hairs, even in her older years.

Nan wore a rose gold wedding ring engraved with her and her husband's initials and the date of their wedding. She also had a half crown given to her by him 'as a token of all I possess' with similar engraving. This engraving must surely have been a bit unusual in 1918, and as Phil is her only granddaughter, she now has Nan's pieces of jewellery, which she treasures dearly.

Nan wore the traditional 'Nana' outfit of dark clothes under a cross-over apron, and dark glasses, and from the few photographs that Phil has of her you can see that she is dressed neatly and was rather tall. Nan was not very active and used a stick to assist her walking, and Phil and Paddy used this stick to try out their 'walking-stick skills', with which Nan was not very impressed!

Nan read the *Cork Examiner* daily and got the *Hollybough* (a Christmas paper published by *The Examiner*) every Christmas. Now when Phil sees the *Hollybough* in the shops she always thinks of Nan and buys it in her memory. Nan took an interest in politics and among her memorabilia were cuttings from newspapers about nationalist activists Kevin Barry, Tomás McCurtain and Terence MacSwiney.

Her mother's death left an enormous void in Phil's life and even to this day she feels the profound impact of a young mother's death and the resulting absolute sense of emptiness in children's lives. Her grandmother, who could not understand why the Lord took the mother of two young children and left her living on at nearly eighty years of age, tried gallantly to help them cope. She was very caring and nurturing. She mashed their potatoes with butter and milk, and when they were sick she gave them a special treat of 'goodie' (white bread soaked in hot milk and sprinkled with sugar). She strove diligently to do their homework with them and helped them in whatever way she could. However, six months later, Nan herself got a stroke and never fully regained her health. She was hospitalised for two weeks and then discharged into their care. She was paralysed on one side of her body and her speech was slurred. This necessitated another big change in Phil's life as Nan now required a lot of care. At ten years of age, Phil was introduced to her first step on a long nursing career. Those were extremely difficult times for all of them, but they coped as best they could and were helped by some good neighbours. After her stroke they cared for Nan for three and a half years with no support services. Phil left for boarding school when she was almost twelve and she remembers Nan being very upset at her leaving – and Phil was equally upset at going away from home for the first time.

Even though her death when it came was expected, it left Phil feeling upset and lonely for a long time. She had only had Nan for twelve years of her life, but Phil feels that her warm, compassionate and caring presence had a long-lasting influence on her life. Nan was there for her when she needed her and that was most important. As Phil's own grandchildren grow up she hopes they will remember her with the same warmth and love that she remembers her Nan.

## Chapter Eighteen

# Granny Woodfort

Many years ago I met Elizabeth at an art class and gradually became aware that this was an amazingly accomplished woman who viewed the world through a very broad lens. Over the years as I got to know her and her family a little better, my sense of wonder at her wide vision and resourcefulness grew. In the face of adversity she displayed an indomitable spirit and I wondered, now that she has gone, what memories and influences she had left behind in the minds of her grandchildren.

Her grandchildren called her Granny Woodfort, giving her the name of the family farmhouse where she lived. As small children they adored their visits to Woodfort. They remember the brightly painted entrance gate and the long driveway, with its view over rolling fields and hills. They were full of anticipation as they parked in her carefully tended, old-world garden, and mounted the many steps to the back door and into her welcoming kitchen.

She knew how to charm small children and she had a 'singing cup' that lived on the dresser in the kitchen and when they arrived down to West Cork from their North Cork home it was the highlight of their visit. She would ensure they each had their turn drinking from it. When the cup left the table and was put to their lips, it would sing! The novelty enthralled them. This is who Granny Woodfort was to them – quirky, a lot of fun, engaging and also practical.

Crafts were her special thing. When each of them was born she put a lot of time and effort into creating beautiful embroidered pictures which had their names on them and a note about its meaning. With one child's name came the quote: 'A merry heart maketh a cheerful countenance', then she'd pick a Biblical verse that felt appropriate to her, for example: 'To walk in the light brings salvation.' She'd focus on that and she'd focus on the child as she worked. For big events or birthdays she always gave thoughtful, home-crafted gifts.

Of her many talented grandchildren three were visually impaired, and Elizabeth was an important person in all her grandchildren's lives. She fanned the seeds of their creativity so that they thrived in the world of music, art and across a wide spectrum of crafts. She would always explain to them what was going on, which was something they greatly appreciated. She also allowed them to be who they were without apology. She always made them feel worthwhile because she always gave them things to do. They came and used her house, so they did something to keep the house going – this wasn't seen as a chore, it was simply returning the love given. When they were young she tucked them into bed with stories about her childhood during the Second World War, when she lived near London, and about the 'Jackie Dorey' people who lived in the woods close-by. *That Takes the Biscuit*, is an anthology of stories by a group of local writers which included Elizabeth's retellings of her wartime days.

She made friends with people who had been traumatised by life and needed to recover. She made her home available to schoolchildren, single mums, extended family members – people who needed a meal or financial support. Emotional stability and kindness were her underlying values, underpinned by her deeply held Christian beliefs.

One grandchild remembers just the two of them going to get a new pup. The puppy was about the size of this child's hand and when Elizabeth was wondering what to call the pup her grandchild, who was visually impaired, asked her, 'What does she look like?', and Elizabeth said that she was the colour of an old penny. So they called the dog Penny to the delight of the little girl.

Their grandmother always had a creative project on the go, be it a seascape painting, an intricate cross-stitch, an elaborate applique, or some delicate silk art. It was rare that a day went by without her working away at one of her undertakings. Yet, after all the hours and hours spent deliberating, planning, preparing and lovingly creating, she gave all her work away. Nearly every single crafted project had a home planned for it before it was even begun. When she made a picture for granddaughter Mandy's twenty-first birthday, it was embroidered with buttons and had pipe-cleaner people sewn on it that Mandy could feel. Mandy thought it was really cool. Granny Woodfort made everything special. For another visually impaired granddaughter, Alice, she made a stylish patchwork handbag – and when she told the local ladies' group what she was making they felt like contributing too, so it became a glorious, colourful assemblage of lace, crochet and knitting, and as tactile and unique as anyone could ever imagine!

She was always up for a bit of fun too and had a really playful side, and would allow her grandchildren to give her weird and wonderful hairstyles and partake in silly photo-shoots. One day she was even daring enough to be persuaded to go on a flimsy rubber donut and be dragged along behind a boat. She shrieked with delight as she whizzed across the water. Not many people in their seventies would sign up for something like that.

When a teenage grandchild got a little too tiresome for their own parents, they would be shipped off to Granny Woodfort for a holiday. They loved these trips. No matter how troublesome they were being at home, they always felt that their grandmother was thrilled and delighted to have them. Days were spent picking apples in the orchard, baking, adventuring or listening to her stories. She would tie handkerchiefs at the end of sticks and fill them with little picnics of rolled up, pinwheel butter sandwiches and they would head off to the fairy fort or down the field for a feast.

In later life she moved to live beside the sea, but for her grandchildren she still retained her Granny Woodfort title. Her house by the sea was a hub for all the family and they arrived like the tide at weekends and withdrew again, leaving way for her midweek activities such as the ladies' crafting group in the local coffee shop, Bible studies, her craft classes for asylum seekers, and visits to some 'elderly people', never counting herself in that number!

Many teenagers might not choose to spend their summers with their Granny, but her grandchildren all gravitated towards Elizabeth. She was easy-going but also proactive in lining up jobs for them. Her teenage grandchildren spent wonderful summers with her, often working in nearby restaurants or on the local strawberry farm in Union Hall. They loved their time there and knew that she enjoyed having them around too for fun and company. She was quite diplomatic too: on one occasion two of the grandchildren had a particularly explosive fight in her presence. They were hurling insults at each other on the stairs, but were suddenly stopped in their tracks by an eruption of her uncontrollable laughter. The entire situation was defused in a matter of moments, with not a word said. She loved her grandchildren and they knew it.

Elizabeth had that ability to get their buy-in through sheer expectation. She expected them to rise to the occasion, to measure up … and they would! And when they did, it was worth it! They would always come through with flying colours and on completion of a task or project they felt a great sense of accomplishment. Her pride in them and in what they produced was a wonderful reward and it was comforting to know that if the notion ever took them again, they'd developed a new skill and they'd be well able for it. Their lack of confidence in their ability would be transformed into a feeling of enhanced self-esteem. They now feel that Elizabeth shaped how they value and perceive themselves and how they form opinions and beliefs about those around them.

Her big skill was getting people involved and she treated everybody equally – as when she made the Glandore quilt with a local group. People were invited to take a patch of material and decorate it, and everyone's contribution was valued, even the old lobster fisherman whose only sewing experience before the age of seventy was mending sails! His square told the wonderful story of cooking in one pot inside another pot, nestled on the bottom of a yawl, and of fishermen covering themselves with the sail when they stayed away overnight. To her everybody had their story to tell and nobody was less or more than she herself was.

They loved how she expected the best from complete strangers too. One of them remembers being offered a summer job – the plan was that some of the grandchildren were going to live with Granny for the summer and work locally. At the last minute, one job fell through. Not to worry, Granny assured the disappointed teenager. She drove up to a neighbour's strawberry farm and explained to the farmer that this child would be an excellent worker and would always put in the muscle, roll up her sleeves and get stuck in, and that she would do an excellent job and that he would not regret taking this worker on. Elizabeth then left and the man realised he was expected to do the needful! She instilled a willingness in people to give things a shot, just roll with it and do their best. The locals used to joke: 'Where do you get your workforce?' and reply was, 'Latvia, Poland and Granny Giles.'

*Aunty Peg's old kitchen table probably dating back to the 1930s. On its last legs!*

*An old, much-treasured Nana ring, with an engraving inside of her wedding date in 1918.*

*This elegant parlour lamp displays the taste and craftsmanship of its time.*

The picture of the Sacred Heart
hung in all homes and recorded the
dates of the births of the children of
the house. Such a picture was often
gifted by mothers to their daughters
for their new homes.

*For some reason,
the Child of Prague,
which was a common
wedding present of the
time, later became a
weather icon used to
influence wedding-day
weather!*

*The set of good china was part of every Nana's household, here surrounded by her other bits and pieces.*

A set of butter knives belonging to Aunty Peg. These too would have been wedding presents of her time.

*This mahogany chest of drawers shows the intricate workmanship that went into the making of these beautiful pieces of furniture.*

Chapter Nineteen

# Nana's Bits and Pieces

The wonky sign over the battered door of the mysterious-looking shop caught my eye: 'Come in and buy what your grandmother threw out'. Who could resist such an invitation? This sign immediately brought a smile to my face because in there I felt was someone with a quirky sense of humour, but who also had a canny insight into the complicated workings of a hoarder's mind. This intriguing invitation into the long, narrow, rabbit-burrow of a shop was irresistible. The sign may have appeared to be an innocent warm welcome, but far more likely was 'cheese in the trap', enticing one into a hoarder's haven promising hours of unadulterated pleasure poking around and exploring. Is there anything more intriguing than the leftover bits and pieces of other people's lives? Looking in, I sensed that in there one could find anything – or maybe nothing. But it was the looking around and searching that was the temptation beyond resistance.

You knew right away that this was not an antique shop or a second-hand furniture shop. It was simply a hurdy-gurdy shop, which is the only name applicable to these indefinable little Aladdin's caves of junk into which the leftovers of many lives eventually find their way. The hurdy-gurdy was an ancient medieval instrument emitting droning sounds, and the word may have come from the Scottish word for 'chaos', which is 'hirdy-girdy'. And in a hurdy-gurdy shop you will usually find organised chaos.

A hurdy-gurdly shop is very different to an antique shop or, indeed, even to a second-hand furniture shop. In an antique shop there will be one perfect period piece in the window and attached to it a price tag at which you swallow hard. You are almost afraid to look because if you do, you might not go in. On entering, there will be an arresting array of perfectly presented, beautifully polished objects, standing or reclining on top of elegant tables or in sparkling inlaid-mahogany glass cases. In there you feel that you should whisper and almost genuflect in awe to all these priceless pieces, and the impeccably dressed assistant usually runs an assessing eye over you to see if you are in the correct money bracket or falling short.

But in a second-hand furniture shop there is often no assistant in sight, and you are lured deeper into a cavernous room where there will be a series of large pieces, reminiscent of polished convent furniture, parish priests' abodes or lord-of-the-manor Big Houses. Here the spacious, well-furnished life of other days is all around you. You can smell the rich aroma of beeswax polish and the years of loving care laboriously lavished on these pieces. The nuns were into high maintenance, as were the dedicated priests' housekeepers, who over the years kept presbyteries in immaculate condition, and the staff in the Big Houses, too, endlessly waxed and polished these pieces. These pieces are remnants of a way of life now gone. In rural Ireland in the past, collectors or well-heeled members of the public watched out for a 'priest's auction' because these auctions would undoubtedly harbour top-quality furniture beautifully maintained by industrious housekeepers who made sure that no grubby woodworm thrust their maggoty heads deep into their well-waxed tables and sideboards.

Once you have yielded to the enticement of one of these showrooms there is usually no visible assistant to cast an eye over you. But as you wander around and come across other addicts appearing and disappearing behind large pieces, a head may appear and cast a disinterested nod in your direction, and you somehow know that this is the guy in charge. And it's usually a guy because moving these weighty pieces around requires male muscle. He knows that if you find what you are looking for, or indeed something unexpected tempts you, then you will find him.

It was in one such place many years ago that Aunty Peg and I came across a mahogany sideboard that caught her fancy. After a lot haggling and good-humoured banter, a price of fourteen pounds was eventually hammered out. Aunty Peg loved a long bargaining session, which she felt was necessary to broker a good deal. She and the affable man in charge enjoyed the wrangling session. Fourteen pounds may make it seem like this sideboard came dirt cheap, but in the 1960s fourteen pounds was a sizeable amount of money and not to be sneezed at.

As a young girl Peg had worked in one of the grand houses and afterwards as an assistant to a parish priest's housekeeper, and in the process had acquired an appreciation of good food, good furniture and fine table linen. So, this sideboard was coming to a good home where it would be well cared for and its deep drawers filled with her best cutlery and good tablecloths, and its many shelves laden with all her best ware. At that time large linen tablecloths, sets of ware or canteens of cutlery were the wedding presents that young couples received on marriage to line their bottom drawer. And for years afterwards the gifts that Peg gave as wedding presents to relatives and friends were the exact same things. She herself was a super housekeeper, keeping everything in glowing order and enjoying the polishing ritual. If you happened to call while this was in progress, she would tell you the story behind each precious acquisition.

She was of her time, but time moves on. Now, the sign over the door of this hurdy-gurdy shop tells the story of the fate of many of those small bits and pieces which, having escaped the ignominious route into a skip, eventually end up in charity shops or shops like this one. In here you could find some interesting items that tell the story of another time, such as the tin box of buttons, the collection of a lifetime of some industrious woman.

Part of the collection on show will usually be an array of clocks that had once graced the mantelpieces of old-world parlours. Some of these clocks have melodious chimes that, as well as telling you the time of day, fill the air with a comforting, musical presence. Here, too, you will find the oak or mahogany eight-day wall clocks that hung on farm-kitchen walls, and are now made redundant by digital timing and fitted kitchens. These wall clocks were not honey-voiced like the mantelpiece clock, but announced the time with an authoritarian, clear strike. They were the time-keepers in the farm kitchens of rural Ireland for decades, and are now to be found in these little cluttered shops – or polished to a new perfection and with a sparkling brass pendulum, in an antique shop, with a price to match. But in the hurdy-gurdy shop you could find a more humble-looking model, with the potential for future restoration. Often these clocks have suffered the indignity of having many coats of paint inflicted on them in an earlier life, but lying in wait beneath these coats of many colours could be the beautiful original wooden coat, waiting to be revealed. And despite the hours of hardship endured removing these tacky coats, eventually comes the unimaginable joy of the final revelation of inlaid mahogany or honey-hued oak. I have experienced this magic more than once! It was as close as I would ever come to discovering a gold nugget on a barren mountain.

Here too are the holy pictures of the past that kept our ancestors sane during tough times and are now stacked shoulder-to-shoulder against mahogany wardrobes and the legs of solid oak tables. Arrayed under the tables are abandoned statues that had once adorned May altars and colourful Child of Prague statues that many a weather-worried bride had put out on the night before her wedding to ward off inclement weather on her big day. And once, on easing open the packed drawer of a tall chest, I found it chock-a-block with family letters and old photographs. When the owners passed away, a disinterested relative who had probably inherited all they possessed had had the house cleared and everything dumped, with no time taken to go through the drawers which might have contained their family history and some valuable little things other relatives might hold dear. These old shops are full of intriguing stories.

So maybe the notice over the door of that shop should have read: 'Come in and see what your grandmother collected and your mother threw out.'

# Chapter Twenty

# The Kitchen Table

I t is falling asunder with fragility but I do not want to let it go, even though holding onto it is pure crazy. It has been with me for so long that some contrary streak in me wants to keep it, feeling the need in some strange way to continue sheltering and honouring its longevity and family history. From a rational point of view this does not make any sense at all, but rational thinking and sentiment do not occupy the same head space – not for me anyway. In fact, sentiment does not belong in any head space as it is not hard-wired into the practical side of the brain and belongs totally in the heart department, where it is sometimes viewed with derision and considered by some as almost a mental weakness. But I think sentiment and nostalgia are offshoots of remembrances, and it seems strange to me that remembrances are quite acceptable whereas senti-

204

ment and nostalgia broker a certain sense of disdain. Now, this old table has nothing to recommend it but sentiment and nostalgia. And to make matters worse, there are two of them! Yes, two tables! One is Aunty Peg's, called after her, and it has its own story. Its twin model was Theresa and Bill's table and is similarly fraught with fragility – it takes its name from Bill because he bought it. They have both spent years as garden furniture in my backyard, one of them as an 'eat outside' table and the other serving as a potting table or sometimes a holder of a mini raised sweet-pea garden. But each table had a precious previous life, and that previous life has its grip on me and will not let go.

These two tables were the kitchen tables in the lives of two much-loved family members: Aunty Peg, who reared my husband and was the Nana in his side of our family, and Bill, a much-loved brother-in-law who air-lifted our first sister to marry, Theresa, out of our family nest. So, the strings attaching these two tables to my heart are not the nails holding the planks of wood together but the memory of the people who once owned them.

Kitchen tables are part of the furniture of our souls. They are the 'altars' from which we partake of the bread of life from the time we are first propped up to one as unsteady babies to the time we are firmly wedged in front of one in wobbly old age. And on the home farm when our turn for the parish Stations came around, our kitchen table became the altar on which Mass was celebrated. For this occasion it was raised at both ends onto the laps of *súgán* chairs to give height and dignity to this special occasion when our family was joined, in spring or autumn, by our neighbours to pray and thank the Lord for the bounties of earth. The practice of the Stations emerged in rural Ireland when the law of the land deemed the celebration of Mass illegal, so Mass went 'underground' onto rocks in valleys and mountains, and then onto kitchen tables.

These old kitchen tables were no lightweights! Nana Ballyduane's long, heavy, narrow table sat in the centre of her big roomy kitchen, and could, without seeming too giant-sized, seat at least a dozen people at harvest time or when the clan gathered. My mother's kitchen table was shorter and broader – kitchen tables at the time were made to suit the requirements of each particular house. Ours was made by a local young craftsman who later went on to become the Minister of Education in the first Irish government. By then, celebrating Mass was no longer illegal, but the Stations custom lingered on because, apart from bringing the light of liturgy into rural homes, it afforded an opportunity for the Church to gather their harvest dues and it gave neighbours a time for thanksgiving and a sociable get together. These tables, as well as sometimes serving as altars, were often the base for the 'miracle of the loaves and fishes' when a little had to go a long way and resourceful mothers and Nanas performed mini miracles, taken for granted by the children and the males in the family.

When the pig was killed in the autumn to provide winter fare, the kitchen table became the butcher's block, first out in the yard for the bloody execution and a few day later for the sectioning and salting of the body parts prior to barrel pickling for longterm preservation. Days later the mincer was attached to the end of the kitchen table and filling the puddings began. These tables were created to serve many purposes and were made to stand firm in all situations.

So, having been reared with these large, commodious kitchen tables it was little wonder that our new brother-in-law, Bill, when he came to purchase his first kitchen table went to the local shop and paid four pounds for a table that was far too large for his new modern house. Years later when I acquired a rambling old house and converted it into a guest house, my sister, Theresa, availed of the opportunity to evict this over-sized table and it found its way to Innis-hannon, where it was warmly received by her grateful, cash-strapped sister. Here it presided for years in the centre of our kitchen where it acted as a base for dishing up fare for dining-room guests and as an eating base for an extending family and a few longterm guests who had become part of us and shared kitchen meals.

After some years, this table grew a bit unsteady on its feet and a wad of cardboard had to be eased under one leg to prevent a landslide of plates, but this slight handicap was compensated for by a sag that developed in the centre where the contents of cups overturned by little hands could be contained in a central well awaiting mop-up. Eventually, however, its infirmities outweighed its usefulness, and it was transferred to a room behind the kitchen where it became the computer base for budding 'Steve Jobs-like' experts. Then one of the guests who had become a much-loved permanent member of the family, and enjoyed woodwork, made a replacement table, capable, like the kitchen tables of old, of handling anything that came its way. In the meantime the computer whizz kids back in the corridor had fled the nest, and Bill's table was no longer required, and so it found its way out into the backyard where it became a garden accessory.

There awaiting it was Aunty Peg's retired kitchen table. In comparison to Bill's, Aunty Peg's table was small, short and sturdy, and had been handmade by Uncle Jacky to fit into a specific space in their little kitchen. Their kitchen was a narrow strip added onto their small sitting room at the back of their village shop. Every time the shop required more space it backed into their living quarters, and then a local handyman added another bit on behind the house. But the size of this small table put no limits to the activity on top. On this table Aunty Peg made cakes, puddings, apple tarts – and if you dropped in while this was going on she simply pushed it all aside and made way for two cups and saucers, put on the kettle and dished out some of what might just have come out of the oven, and joined you in the savouring. So this little table did much work in its day.

When they were evicted to my backyard these two tables must have then looked at each other and said: And this is our thanks after our long and faithful service; what ungrateful wretches people are! Or maybe they were delighted and said: Well, isn't it great to be out here in the fresh air where we can grow old in peace and quiet together.

Out in the backyard their reincarnation began. Because Bill's table was the bigger and fitted in beautifully in a sunny south-facing corner by the garden shed, it was the ideal base for long boxes of sweet-pea seeds that when summer came could take off and climb up the latticed side of the shed, and there was still enough space in front for impromptu potting. This worked wonderfully and for years Bill's old table had its special place in the sun.

Aunty Peg's table, being shorter and more mobile, was parked right behind the back door which made it very convenient from the nearby kitchen, so transferring food to it was very easy. Aunty Peg's table became our main outdoor eating area. For some strange reason, when Jacky made this table the three wide timber planks on the top had never got attached to the four wide solid legs beneath it – I never could figure that one out, but maybe he knew not the day nor the hour when Peg, who could be a trifle unpredictable, might have a change of plan and such a table was much more adaptable for movement. In any case I found this to be so, and if a change of location was desirable or movement for winter storage into the garden shed was needed you simply whipped off the three planks, upended the four legs and away you went. And when it was stationary behind the back door and draped in a giant-sized oilcloth – which for special occasions could be covered with a fancier one – it was the picture of stability.

These two old tables should have been replaced years ago by two slick new weather-resistant models, but new ones would not have brought the light of two well-loved people into my backyard. I enjoyed having these two old friends behind my back door where they somehow added an extra dimension to days outside, whether I was lazing around, working or simply looking up at the sky, watching the birds and the occasional plane from nearby Cork airport pass overhead.

But unfortunately, today Bill's table decided to finally give up the ghost. This was not a sudden death because a few years back the leg that had always been a problem gave way at the knee and the bottom section had to be removed, and so all the other legs had to follow suit as a knee replacement was not an option owing to the age and fragility of the entire body. This four-legged amputation led to a sudden sinking to a lower position, ruling it out as a potting table, but for the sweet-peas it simply meant a higher climb.

However, today this old friend decided that it had reached a place called 'stop'. The sag in the middle decided to bottom out, which necessitated a hasty removal of every-thing on board. The time had come to finally call it a day, so I removed the all-encompassing oilcloth that had been holding it together and shrouding its senility. Then, unex-pectedly, I was joined by a son who could be handy with a hammer, and slowly and regretfully the frail body joints were eased apart and we bore them up into the garden to create a bug bank where the timbers could decay in their own time and return to the earth from whence they had come.

Aunty Peg's sturdier table is still standing and will live to provide sustenance for another while yet. I know that this does not make any practical sense, but then sentiment and nostalgia were never meant to do so.

# Chapter Twenty One

# The Last Dance

In this salutation to the Nanas I hope that you found little remembrances of your own Nana. These women deserve our acknowledgement and respect for the values that they nurtured and passed on. In a male-dominated world they coped with much that would not be tolerated today, but despite that they succeeded in nurturing a lot to be admired and acknowledged: a philosophy inherited from female ancestors, but also the wisdom of their own time.

Their world was sustained by an acceptance of a divine power greater than themselves, a respect for the natural world, the importance of the family support unit and a belief in the work ethic which resulted in the therapy of doing.

Back then the hearth truly was the heart of the home – the place for cooking, water-heating, sitting to chat, knitting, darning, storytelling, social gatherings, even rearing the runt of the pig litter and taking care of a baby lamb until he was strong enough to join the rest of the flock. Everything happened around that fire. Its warmth spread into all the activities of the home and became Nana's corner, when in her later years she sat beside it and carried on all her business from there.

My fire is not the open fire of our Nanas' era but it has its own magnetic embracing ambience and over the years ours has been a long-lasting and warm love affair, that began with its arrival into my life when a safe haven of retreat was needed in a house where no corner was quiet and restful. Then the quiet room we christened the 'seomra ciúin' came into being, with its warm-hearted, comfortable fireplace. But, unfortunately, now it has to go! Environmental concerns have made me feel guilty about lighting my fire. Turf and coal are now a no-no and have to be consigned to the past. So, sadly, this is going to be my last Christmas beside my old-fashioned friendly fire that I have known and loved for many years. Could this be the end of the 'Nana by the fire'? Have we reached the end of an era? Am I the last in that long line? A sobering thought indeed!

In the New Year I will say goodbye to my fire, with many warm, regretful remembrances. Sitting by it down through the years, watching its imagery and absorbing its warmth has healed me through bereavement and other family upsets. A warm fire is a therapeutic companion. Its soothing heat is a healing solace. But as I sit by it now, the song that keeps playing at the back of my brain is the old Jim Reeves number

'He'll Have to Go'. This was a smoothly flowing melody from about fifty years ago that we all danced to during the showband era. Jim Reeves, who was the Garth Brooks of his day, had a voice like melting honey that helped massage many romances into being. It transformed basic ballrooms into heavenly havens. It was heart-warming and comforting, as indeed was my beloved fire. But the ballrooms are gone, Jim Reeves is gone – and now it is time for my fire to go as well. The time has come to say goodbye. Environmental warning bells are clanging loudly and we all have to make an effort to reduce our carbon footprint. I too need to do my bit.

Like many of my generation and those before us, and maybe indeed a generation after us, we were all reared around an open fire. There was even a programme on Raidio Eireann long ago, hosted by Joe Linnane, called 'Around the Fire', from where many a song poured forth into country kitchens all over Ireland as we sat around the fire. One song that always comes to my mind from that era is the wonderful voice of Seán O Siocháin singing 'The Boys of Barr na Sráide as we hunted for the Wran'.

But in truth, though that open fire strove gallantly to keep us warm, it did very little to warm us or the house around us. The odds were stacked against it because if you stood in under our enormous chimney breast in the home farm and looked up the chimney you could see the sky. So at night we were actually trying to warm the stars twinkling above! But at Christmas this chimney came into its own as far as I was concerned because it took very little stretch of a child's imagination to visualise Santa making his way down along it on Christmas night, and there were even iron brads sticking out along the way to help him make it down. I doubt that these were inserted with that particular job in mind, but for a child at Christmas that's exactly the purpose that they were made to serve.

But in fairness to that open fire, the task of keeping us and the house around us warm was beyond achievability because every night cold winds whipped in under the doors, and on stormy nights all the windows rattled in protest against the onslaught. But, despite the efforts of prevailing weather conditions to counteract the warming affects of the fire, every night we all gathered around it anyway and it did succeed in dispelling the worst of the cold, assisted by jute farm bags laid along the bottoms of the doors to prevent at least some of the determined wind from getting in. And, in reality, this fire was multi-purpose because it also provided the only cooking facility in the house. In every country kitchen the open fire was overhung by an iron crane off which dangled all sizes of kettles and pots, and out of all these came the sustenance to keep a farm family fed and watered. It needed to be large and wide open to accomplish all that. Whatever about its efficiency, it was definitely the heart of the home. We gathered around it every night to talk, and tell each other stories, and exchange the happenings of the day – and sometimes our mother caught up with her darning as we children did our lessons. And it had another dimension as well in that it provided a sheltered corner where Nana, at the end of her days, could sit in the midst of the family and mind the baby of the house.

For her last twenty years our Nana sat by her own fire and ran the kitchen, the farm and, in her opinion, the country as well. At seventy, she had decided that it was time to fold up her tent and move on. But either there was no room on the departure bus or God, whom she regularly called to order, decided that he had enough on his hands besides our Nana so he kept her in the waiting room for another twenty years. But once she got accustomed to being in her chimney corner she settled down there and used it as her social centre and family control tower.

But the fire in our '*seomra ciúin*' is a far cry from those old-fashioned farm kitchen fires, and it certainly did not face the same challenges. Our iron grate was fitted over a baxi box, which is a little tin box fitted beneath the grate to catch the ashes and so remove the need for too frequent emptying. I thought that this was very modern, innovative thinking, until Mrs C acidly informed me that she had one in London years earlier during the war years. This grate was set into a solid wrought-iron surround that had been preserved from Aunty Peg's old house and then surrounded by an oak wooden mantelpiece that had been acquired from a restorer, who had laughingly informed me that he was shifting those mantelpieces out of one end of the South Mall in Cork and putting them in at the other end! Such are the varied customs of changing times.

Our 'seomra ciúin' was set aside as a quiet retreat in a very busy household. There was to be no TV or phone connection in there, which led to comments from certain family members that nobody would ever go in there. These sceptics, however, were proved entirely wrong, and the appeal and the tranquility in there, and the warmth of that fire, drew people in around it like a magnet. On the wall above it hung an old eight-day wind-up ticking clock, and to sit beside that fire and listen to the ticking clock calmed the most bothered minds.

Over the years garden trees that came aground in stormy weather found their way as blocks into the depths of that fire where they were licked warm by sods of blazing turf gifted to us from a bog in Kerry. For me the very best present at Christmas was a bag of turf or a trailer of logs that sometimes came my way. The sight of a pile of timber blocks heaped up in the backyard always caused me to think of where they had come from and their journey back out to the compost heap where, as ashes, they would once again blend back into the earth and become part of another cycle of new growth. In the fire they talked to me and licked me whole when I was bruised by life or bleeding with grief. Tim, the chimney cleaner who came every year, was a trusted and dependable carer of my chimney.

Recently, to ease my environmental conscience, and, trying desperately to hold onto my old friend, I have moved to using smokeless coal and kiln-dried wood. But now I know that environmentally this is not enough – and so my

The Nana

friend the fire has to go. True for Shakespeare: 'Conscience makes cowards of us all'. But in this instance it is also making me more environmentally conscious and fostering a responsible approach to the welfare of the earth.

And so, on our last nights together, as my friend the fire and I sit listening to the ticking clock I will look back with appreciation and gratitude to all the ease and comfort it has afforded me over the years. But at the back of my mind a replacement plan is forming! In the New Year I will make my way to an old-fashioned little draper's shop high up in the hills of North Cork and purchase a big supply of warm Nana knickers. Because one of the many skills our Nanas demonstrated and passed on was the art of coping astutely and gracefully with whatever came their way. And so – on go the Nana knickers!

218

The súgán chair was part of the kitchen requirements and these were made and súgáned locally, indeed often by the man of the house.

This old man started off as part of a calendar and was later framed to hang over many mantelpieces. It was gifted to me by an old friend when I expressed a liking for it.

PLAYER'S NAVY CUT

HERO

TOBACCO

AND
CIGARE

*This was a mirror cum advertisement for cigarettes that hung in our old shop.*

A little oven that was used for cooking bits and pieces and now enjoyed by the birds in my garden.

The enamel bucket was the holder of milk and also used to bring water from the well; the enamel or tin pan was used for making the bread.

*Free-range hens were the norm and the egg money was part of the female farm income.*

Holding the baby – my youngest grandchild.

*The much-loved fire
that for many years
warmed my heart
and home.*

*Most illnesses were treated at home,*
*but when that was not possible the*
*Cork Nanas felt that 'The Bons' was*
*the next best thing!*

TEL. No. 21405

CK STREET.

Cork, January 31st, 1959

*D. Broderick,* M.P.S.I., M.I.A.D.O.

Pharmacist to Bon Secours Hospital, College Road, Cork.

To Mrs. Julia Healy, Room 58

Bon Secours Home,

Bengour, Newcestown, Co. Cork.

ACCOUNTS PAYABLE AT THE OFFICE, BON SECOURS HOSPITAL.

| 1959 | | Seconal Tabs. grs. 1½ | | £ — |
|------|----|------------------------|---|-----|
| Jan. | 31 | | | |

*This tray and brush were used for gathering up breadcrumbs off the tablecloth.*

*Perfume was a luxury and came in very small bottles, sometimes carried around in handbags.*

The arrival of tap water
removed the hard task of
drawing water by bucket
from the well.

*Knitting went on in most households and all drapers' shops carried a great selection of hanks of wool, which then had to be wound into balls.*

Lamps were fuelled by oil, out of
which came the wick that could be
raised or lowered by turning the little
wheel at the side.

*Leatherwork was often taught at night classes, and Celtic designs were much saught after.*

enthroned in this home on the 22nd day of June 1966

ers of the family, present or absent, living or dead.

o recognize Jesus as our Lord and Master. We acce

nd of His Holy Church; we express our horror at th

individuals, by families and by nations; we condems

ge, and finally we submit with our whole heart an

ther the Pope.

s confers on us by coming to take up His abode v

r in our home and in our hearts.

s    Miceál, Donnca Zearóid
     Seán, Diarmuid agus        } Childre
     Lena Síle Mairéad.
7. O'Riordan  C.C.

*The Sacred Heart picture was gifted*
*to me by my mother, a custom of the*
*time. My husband, Gabriel, added*
*the family names in the old Irish*
*script which he loved.*

*This little guy looks as if he's enjoying himself. I picked him up in a hurdy-gurdy shop.*

This statue of Maria Goretti belonged to my sister Ellen, and depicts kindness and gentleness.

# *Other books by Alice Taylor:*

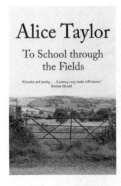

Alice Taylor

To School through
the Fields

'Evocative and moving ... A journey every reader will treasure.'
*Boston Herald*

Alice Taylor
A Cocoon with a View

A BOOK OF COMFORT FOR ALL TIMES

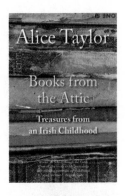

Alice Taylor

Books from
the Attic

Treasures from
an Irish Childhood

Alice Taylor

Tea and Talk

Alice Taylor

And Life Lights Up
MOMENTS THAT MATTER

Alice Taylor

The Women

Alice Taylor

Do You Remember?

Alice Taylor

As Time Goes By

Alice Taylor

Tea for One
A Celebration of Little Things

*See the O'Brien Press website,*
*www.obrien.ie, for a full list*